PARADOXES OF CHRISTIAN
FAITH AND LIFE

Paradoxes of Christian Faith and Life

by

RICHARD HOLLOWAY

MOWBRAY
LONDON AND OXFORD

ISBN 0 264 67005 1

First published 1984
by A.R. Mowbray & Co. Ltd.,
Saint Thomas House, Becket Street,
Oxford, OX1 1SJ

Typeset by Set Fair Limited
Printed in Great Britain by Biddles Ltd, Guildford.

British Library Cataloguing in Publication Data

Holloway, Richard
Paradoxes of christian faith and life.
1. Suffering—Religious aspects—Christianity 2. Sex—Religious
aspects—Christianity
I. Title
231'.8   BV4908
ISBN 0-264-67005-1

For Martin Shaw
beloved friend

Acknowledgements

As usual, I have to begin by thanking my secretary, Martha Mitchell, for her unfailing graciousness and efficiency in preparing these pages for the printer. I must also thank Rusty Miller for his assistance in preparing the manuscript and for many other kindnesses. William Purcell urged me to put these pages together and therefore bears some responsibility for their appearance, though he bears no responsibility for any of the ideas expressed.

The Church of the Advent
30 Brimmer Street, Boston   R.H.

The author and publisher wish to express their thanks to the following for permission to reproduce material of which they are the authors, publishers or copyright holders.

A.D. Peters & Co. Ltd for an extract from *The Towers of Trebizond* by Rose Macaulay.

Faber and Faber Publishers for four lines from 'Little Gidding' from *Four Quartets* by T.S. Eliot.

David Higham Associates Limited for an extract from *Descent into Hell* by Charles Williams (Faber and Faber); and for an extract from *The Poems* by Dylan Thomas (J.M. Dent & Sons Ltd).

Harvard University Press for an extract from *Jowett* by Geoffrey Faber.

George Allen & Unwin (Publishers) Ltd for an extract from *Christianity at the Crossroads* by George Tyrrell.

Random House, Inc. for 'The Excesses of God' from *Selected Poems* by Robinson Jeffers.

A.P. Watt Ltd, Literary Agents, on behalf of Michael Yeats and Macmillan, London, Ltd for an extract of fourteen lines from 'The Second Coming' from *Collected Poems of W.B. Yeats*.

The Society of Authors as the literary representatives of the Estate of A.E. Housman, and Jonathan Cape Ltd, publishers of A.E. Houseman's *Collected Poems*, for an extract from Poem XL from 'A Shropshire Lad'.

If any copyright has been unwittingly transgressed, we make sincere apologies and will acknowledge any such oversights in future editions.

Biblical quotations are from the Revised Standard Version.

Contents

INTRODUCTION

The Rock and the River   3

PART ONE

SUFFERING: AN EXPLORATION

1. The Land of Lost Content   15
2. The Valley of Decision   26
3. A Death in Jerusalem   39

PART TWO

THE CHRISTIAN AND THE SEXUAL REVOLUTION

4. What Is Sex For?   57
5. The Christian Answer   72
6. Putting Asunder   80

PART THREE

PRIEST TO THE WORLD

7. Looking Towards Jesus   93
8. The Perfect Priest   105
9. The Folly of Preaching   117

EPILOGUE

Paradise Row   131
Notes   142

INTRODUCTION

The Rock and the River

For anyone who likes a quiet and changeless life, the Christian Church in the last quarter of the twentieth century is a disquieting and irritating institution. Most men and women require some sort of abiding security round which to build their lives. This is partly because we feel ourselves, anyway, to be victims of natural and historical processes that bear us away, and as the river pushes us on, we look for certain things to cling to, we long for some things that will abide. One of the historical functions of religion has been to provide this element of stability and continuity for lives that are threatened by the unavoidable pressures of change. This is one reason why religious institutions tend to be conservative and resistant to change. Of course, they do change, but usually at a stubbornly slow pace and in a way that retains a sense of real continuity with the past. According to certain sociologists, it is this very conservatism that makes religious institutions so valuable to human beings. Threatened, as we are, by the flux of time and change, the apparently timeless certainties of religious institutions provide us with important elements of continuity which enable us to absorb and adapt to the tyrannous pressures of change. As such, these institutions fulfil what is called 'an integrating function': they enable us to make necessary adaptations to change, while retaining a real sense of permanent identity. Change unmitigated by stability would cause disintegration, just as utterly unchanging stability would lead to the rigidity of death. Just as deep-sea divers observe a method of rising to the surface that reduces the pressure on their lungs and heart and allows the body to adapt to the changing pressure in a gradual way, so

3

do certain institutions, such as the Church, allow us to adapt to the pressure of change in a way that minimizes the shock to our system, though discomfort there always is. The pace of change is itself always a matter of dispute, but very few people today would argue for change unmodified by the hold of the past. The really new element in the current situation is that the pace of change has become almost impossible to adapt to in the old, steady way. It is as though a diver were being pulled to the surface at supersonic speed, resulting in a serious case of 'the bends'. Alvin Toffler coined the phrase 'future shock' to describe this contemporary trauma. For many people, the most shocking element in the present situation is that the Church, far from helping people to adapt wisely to change at a healthy pace, has itself become a source of pressure. The rock to which they clung in the river of time is moving and breaking into fragments. There is hardly an aspect of the Church's life in which there are no pressures towards change. The physical arrangement of our church buildings is changing — in the Roman Catholic Church they changed virtually overnight! Our liturgies and prayer books are changing. Our forms of ecclesiastical administration are changing. The very shape and scope of the ordained ministry is changing. These changes might be absorbed as superficial, as alterations to the form of the Church and not to its substance, were it not for the presence of more profound pressures upon the Church that seem to threaten its very substance and meaning. The Church's understanding of the faith which it is its task to keep, is itself under severe pressure from theologians. And nowhere is the pressure for change more clamant and bitter than in the area of morals. The Church's traditional teaching about marriage and divorce, about sexual relations, and about the meaning of the sanctity of human life are all under a state of siege from within and without. There is a lot of evidence to indicate that this relentless pressure towards change has produced a state of chronic anxiety in Christians.

4

America is, for the West, the laboratory of cultural change, and the pressures there have led, for instance, to a dramatic polarization of Christian opinion. Unfortunately, there is no cosmic umpire who can blow a timely whistle and allow us an interlude in which to regain our breath and adjust our tactics. We are relentlessly borne along. There are, of course, no lack of confident voices yelling above the scrum, some calling us back to the past and its timeless truths, others calling us confidently to follow them over the cliff into the changeful future. Many of us, alas, are not sure which way to go and are furiously jostled to the right and to the left.

Now, while the pressure of change is admittedly unprecedented today, it will be of some comfort and instruction to think briefly about past changes in Christian attitudes. Many moral attitudes that we take for granted today were once the subject of bitter dispute among Christians, such as the ancient debate over usury. The charging of interest by Jews to their own people was forbidden by the Law. 'If you lend money to any of my people with you who is poor, you shall not be to him as a creditor, and you shall not exact interest from him' (Exod. 22.25). 'You shall not lend upon interest to your brother, interest on money, interest on victuals, interest on anything that is lent for interest. To a foreigner you may lend upon interest, but to your brother you shall not lend upon interest . . .' (Deut. 23.19-20). In the early Church the taking of interest came to be regarded as unlawful, and it was formally condemned by the Third Lateran Council in 1179. It was for this reason that European Jews developed their reputation as money-lenders in the Middle Ages. G.G. Coulton pointed out that to them was reserved the right to lend money: '. . . if the Jew is to be here at all and do any good, he must be allowed to do things that are forbidden to Christians, notably to take interest on money lent . . .'[1] By this rather hypocritical device, the commercial development of medieval Europe was furthered. In practice, as commerce developed, interest payment in business came to be justified, and it prepared the foundation for the rise of European capitalism. Today we take all this for granted, and many opponents of the new morality are staunch defenders of that very capitalism which was once the subject of such dispute. So does the wheel turn.

The Church's attitude to contraception is also instructive. As long as sexual intercourse was regarded as an entirely reproductive function, artificial methods of birth control were forbidden by Christian thought. Gradually, however, there developed a concern about over population and, at the same time, a new attitude to the sexual act within marriage emerged, which saw it as a relational act and not just a productive function. Under these twin pressures the Churches of the Reformation modified their attitude to contraception and Christians were permitted to practice it. It is still, of course, officially condemned by the Roman Catholic Church, but a practical and theoretical consensus in its favour has silently emerged among Catholic laity in the West.

But not all moral revisionism is in a permissive direction. Here the Christian attitude to slavery is instructive. Christ came preaching the liberation of captives and thus provided the Church with a radical theological criticism of slavery, but, in practice, as the Church developed within the Roman Empire it took for granted the persistence of slavery and itself became a slave holder. It was not until the Congress of Vienna, in 1814, that the Christian powers of Europe brought an end to the slave trade. In America the debate was even more bitter than in Europe, and Christians used the Bible both to attack and defend slavery. It took the American Civil War to end slavery in America, in 1863, though its bitter legacy still persists.

If it is hard for a Christian today to understand how the Church could ever have justified slavery, it is just as hard to accept some of the historical attitudes to class that

Christians have evinced. The sad, though perhaps inevitable, fact is that Christians tend to pick up their social attitudes from the societies in which they live. This is even true of moral reformers, who tend to reflect the current interests of the avant-garde. For centuries, the Church accepted the wide inequalilty that existed between the classes in Europe. It is also true that Christians were in the forefront of the reform movement that improved the working and living conditions of the poor, but the extraordinary fact remains that Christians of considerable sensitivity and goodwill were able to accept the horrors of child-labour and insanitary overcrowding that typified the lot of the poor until not very long ago. Every piece of philanthropic reform, whether in the field of organized labour, or the factory inspection acts, or in the gradual and grudging widening of the suffrage to include all adult citizens, has been both advocated and opposed on Christian grounds. Today we take for granted that it is monstrous to allow young boys to climb into chimneys to sweep them, and that it is a flagrant abuse of human rights to flog soldiers for minor infractions of duty; yet both of these were time-honoured institutions in Britain until the last century.

This historical retrospect seems to teach several lessons. The first is that not all moral revision has been in a direction that weakens the ethical rigour of the Christian life. It is dangerous to use words like 'progress' in talking of these matters, but there is some evidence to support the thesis that in certain areas of morality there has been a specific translation into law of much that is implicit in the Christian understanding of human nature. If there has been a weakening in the area of private and particularly sexual morality, there has been a strengthening of the Christian ethic in many significant social areas. There may even be some sort of moral ratio at work here, whereby private rigour increases public slackness and vice versa. I do not want to lay too much emphasis upon any of this, but it is too simple to say that 'we're going to the dogs'. The truth is, we've always lived close to the kennels. It may be easier for the Christian to commit fornication with his immediate neighbour today; it is much more difficult to exploit him economically or politically. There has been gain and loss, what accountants call 'a wash'. Lord Macaulay remarked upon this phenomenon in 1827:

> Every age and every nation has certain characteristic vices, which prevail almost universally, which scarcely any person scruples to avow, and which even rigid moralists but faintly censure. Succeeding generations change the fashion of their morals, with the fashion of their hats and their coaches; take some other kind of wickedness under their patronage, and wonder at the depravity of their ancestors.[2]

The second thing to note is that it is extremely difficult for Christians to avoid conformity to the surrounding society. The glory of the prophet is his ability to rise above this smothering ambience and see moral issues in clear, uncluttered terms. For most of us, alas, this is not the way it is at all. We pick up our attitudes from those around us, often unconsciously, and, if we are Christians, we often seek some kind of Christian validation for attitudes we may hold on other grounds. This is a dismaying thing to recognize in oneself, and it is not immediately apparent what one can do about it. The only certain way to preserve an institution from the erosions of change is to keep it in a cultural ghetto where it cannot interact with the prevailing views of the surrounding society. This can, of course, be done quite effectively. A good example is provided by the Hasidic Jewish community in Brooklyn, which manages to preserve a way of life and thought that is remarkably unaffected by the secular culture of eastern America. But even here there are tensions, as the novels of Chaim Potok so sensitively describe. At various times and in various places Christians have had, perforce, to live such a ghetto existence. It has not, however, been the tradition of Western Christianity. It is true that the social tradition of the Western Church has reflected many changes, from a desire to dominate society in some periods to an apparent longing to take all its order from society in others. What has been common has been the conviction that Church and society must interact closely, because the Church exists for the sake of the world in which it is set.

In the case of established Churches the temptation has always been to provide a Christian legitimation for the state. For example, the Anglican Church throughout its history has been a kind of political litmus paper. While it is true that it has always contained within its rather slack embrace people of almost every political persuasion, it has tended, in its official aspect, to reflect the going fashion in politics and social thought. It still does. And here there are some agreeable ironies to savour. Once it was accurate enough to describe the Church of England as the Conservative party at prayer. Now it would probably be safer to describe it as the Social Democratic party at Mass. There has been a tip towards the left in social and political thought and fashion in the West in recent years, and this, as we might expect, has been accurately reflected in the Christian Church. The pattern seems to be straightforward. Significant shifts in ideas occur when society's opinion formers succeed in naturalizing ideas that were once alien. This usually happens first among intellectuals. Gradually, a great deal of pressure is built up against the old conviction that is under attack by the new idea which is to take its place. There is always a spirited resistance on the part of some, but the resistance is doomed at the point where the new and more assertive point of view is accepted by the majority, even where it is technically against either state or ecclesiastical law. In the case of the state, there is usually a period when the old law is 'inoperative', and this is followed by the promulgation of a new law that permits what the old

9

forbade. This has usually been the pattern of change in sexual morals, but it also tends to be the case in attitudes to economics and class. In a surprisingly short time, therefore, the previously unmentionable can become the currently fashionable. There are enormous dangers for Christians in this situation, surrounded, as we are, by insidious and seductive pressures to conform to or legitimate the standards of the society in which we are set.

Some years ago Martin Thornton wrote an interesting book called *The Rock and the River*, in which he tried to do justice to both the firmness of Christian faith and the fluidity of human history in which it is set. How do we cling to the rock and flow with the river? The question has something of the paradoxical power of a Zen saying. The answer cannot simply be: 'Come out of the river and cling only to the rock'; or, 'Dive off the rock and into the river' — though polemicists tend to do one or the other. Christians, by the mysterious impossibility of faith, have to do both at the same time. After all, Paul described a similar absurdity when he talked about the rock that followed the children of Israel in the wilderness. Maybe our rock does the same, swimming after us as we flounder around in the river of time. I have described these reflections as 'paradoxes' because each section, in its own way, reflects a strong desire to hold to the rock and swim in the river, sometimes even against the current. For years I have been haunted by two epigrams. The first comes from F.D. Maurice by way, I believe, of Coleridge and Aristotle: 'Men are usually right in what they affirm and wrong in what they deny'. The second comes from Charles Williams and it has a mysterious power: 'This also is thou; neither is this thou'. I think Williams meant that every truth, true though it be, has to be balanced immediately by the truth that is opposite it. F.D. Maurice was trying to say something similar, I think. Affirmations are more inclusive than denials, for they are better able to contain their opposites. In other words, it is better to affirm than to deny, to say what you

10

believe or hold, without succumbing to the ancient temptation to engage in consequential denunciation of the affirmations of others. Of course, paradox reigns here, too, for affirmations sometimes carry along the need to oppose dangerous error. Even so, the doctrine holds, I believe. On the whole, it is better to affirm than to deny, to know what you believe than to attack what you don't believe. People will usually listen if you tell them what you think you see from where you stand. They are understandably irritated if you tell them that they cannot possibly be seeing what they claim to see from where *they* stand. This is where many theologians miss the point. They do not seem content to set forth the extent or limit of their own sights, they must be forever telling us why their current range of vision must become the norm. Fortunately, they change their spectacles as often as the rest of us.

I know that I often sin against Maurice and Williams in my tone. I try to excuse myself by claiming that I only deny those who reject my affirmations! Well, I know that won't do. However, I hope it can be said that I have at least tried to affirm more than I deny. I have noticed that something of the flavour of these paradoxes and antinomies has crept into my wrestling with the themes in this book. As I said, that's why I called them paradoxes. However, 'explorations' might have been a better description, remembering T.S. Eliot's famous paradox. It comes to the same thing in the end.

> We shall not cease from exploration
> And the end of our exploring
> Will be to arrive where we started
> And know the place for the first time.[3]

This book is not a connected narrative, but neither is it a collection of rags and patches stitched into some kind of quilt. It is largely a collection of conferences, all on different themes but all sharing an underlying unity of approach. Part One, Suffering: An Exploration, was

11

delivered as a series of lectures at Christ Church, Cambridge, Massachusetts, in Lent 1983. Part Two, The Christian and the Sexual Revolution, started life as a series of sermons at the Church of the Advent, Boston, Massachusetts, in Lent 1982. Part Three, Priest to the World, was largely delivered at the Australian Catholic Renewal Conference in Melbourne, in May 1983. The chapter on The Folly of Preaching was originally published in *Theology* in October 1980. The epilogue, Paradise Row, was delivered at Melbourne at the conference already referred to.

PART ONE

SUFFERING:
AN EXPLORATION

1. The Land of Lost Content

One summer morning when I was reading Morning Prayer, I got locked on to the last three verses of Psalm 39. I was on vacation. When I'm on vacation I pick my way slowly through the psalms in Latin, because I find it more conducive to meditation. I'm not in any rush, so I can linger here and there. Sometimes I stop altogether, because something in the verse holds me. That's what happened on this occasion.

Ad lacrimas meas ne obsurdescas;	Be not deaf to my tears;
Quoniam advena ego sum apud te,	For I am a stranger with thee,
Peregrinus sicut omnes patres mei.	A pilgrim like all my fathers.
Avertere a me, ut refrigerer,	Look away from me, that I may
Priusquam abeam et non sim	be refreshed,
amplius	Before I depart and be no more.

Some of the words jumped out at me: *advena*, a stranger, a visitor; *peregrinus*, a pilgrim, a wanderer. The Psalmist sees himself as a homeless wanderer, passing through God's territory, and he asks God to let him be, to turn a blind eye, to let him camp for a bit on the edge of town that he may refresh himself before wandering off again into the dark. I felt enormous compassion for the Psalmist and a strong fellow-feeling. I was hearing one of the genuine voices of the Old Testament, and it resonated with my own experience. Part of me is still very much with this wistful, defensive wanderer across God's territory, who is not sure of a welcome and, anyway, just wants to be left alone for a night to rest up before moving off again. We find almost the same image in Job 14:

Man that is born of a woman is of few days, and full of trouble. He comes forth like a flower, and withers; He flees like a shadow, and continues not.

And dost thou open thy eyes upon such a one and bring him into judgement with thee? Who can bring a clean thing out of an unclean? There is not one. Since his days are determined, and the number of his months is with thee, and thou hast appointed his bounds that he cannot pass, look away from him, and desist, that he may enjoy, like a hireling, his day.

There it is again: 'Look away from him, and desist, that he may enjoy, like a hireling, his day.' The tired, stubborn wistfulness of the man who wishes God would leave him alone, stop bullying him, and just let him enjoy his brief day. God is back there somewhere, it seems, like a powerful rancher, trying to chase the Indians off his land or organize them into tidy reservations. He's got everything he wants there, back at the ranch: why, then, does he bother this poor wanderer, skulking round the end of time, trying to grab a moment of rest and pleasure here and there, before fleeing away like a shadow?

There is a gentle, almost pagan, melancholy in these Old Testament protests. They talk of the transience and vulnerability of human nature. 'All flesh is grass', the Psalmist says elsewhere. You can't expect much of grass. Let it enjoy its brief day. Who can grudge such migrants their fleeting pleasure? Why trouble them with the disciplines of uncertain eternity? They come forth like flowers and wither. 'And dost thou open thy eyes upon such and bring them into judgement with thee?' Leave them, God, leave them alone. They did not ask to be born. Why trouble their dust with your dreams and demands? Let them enjoy, like hirelings, their day. Many of them find it brief and

16

bittersweet enough, shot through with a strange sor-
rowing — a private sorrow, but one other wanderers know
well.

I know that sense of strange regret very well, and I know
I am not alone. It seems the human wanderer in his brief
march across time finds the pleasures of his journey
increasingly tinged with a mysterious sorrow. For some
reason, he cannot enjoy, like a hireling, his day, because
something haunts him in spite of himself. Increasingly, he
feels he has lost something, as A.E. Housman suggested:

> Into my heart on air that kills
> From you far country blows:
> What are those blue remembered hills,
> What spires, what farms are those?

> That is the land of lost content,
> I see it shining plain,
> The happy highways where I went
> And cannot come again.[1]

The killing sense of loss and regret is made of many
things, but the most potent ingredient is surely the passing
of time. We may not notice this when we are young. Time is
full of promise, then, and we are impatient to snatch its
glittering prizes, so we leap aboard. 'And thus the whirligig
of time brings in his revenges', as Shakespeare tells us in
Twelfth Night. Shakespeare, in fact, is a good place to begin
in contemplating the deceits of time.

> When to the sessions of sweet silent thought
> I summon up remembrance of things past,
> I sigh with lack of many a thing I sought,
> And with old woes new wail my dear times' waste:
> Then can I drown an eye, unus'd to flow,
> For precious friends hid in death's dateless night,

And weep afresh love's long since cancell'd woe,
And moan the expense of many vanish'd sight.[2]

The poet's vocation, it seems brings with it a piercing
sense of devouring time. Dylan Thomas had it. Two of his
lines have haunted for me years. He mourns,

Wild men who caught and sang the sun in flight,
And learn, too late, they grieved it on its way.[3]

Nothing lasts! Isn't that the knowledge that surprises us
into sudden tenderness and weakens the harshness of our
judgements? We love all these because they die, or we
remember, too late, that they were dying all the time. We
feel like haunted creatures. Is that true? Certainly, some of
us are haunted, *I* am haunted, haunted by time and dying
and a strange sense of demand that troubles me, yet never
fully explains itself. Can God, if there is a God, really be
bothered by my failures and frailties, when he knows I am
dying and mourning all my life long?

There's a road I know, from a deep hollow by a river up
to the top of a rise, and I would turn at the top and see a
range of green hills in the distance, and the beauty of it
always made me sad and lonely, made me mourn, though
my children played around me. I think it was because my
mother used to tell me of a walk up another hill she took us
on as children, and we ceased to be children and the
walking ceased, but she was never happier, she said, than in
those days. Roads are like that. They suggest partings, ways
we can never come again. Or they remind us of roads not
taken, possible pasts, alternative though now impossible
histories that might have been happier, stories where we
might have found the land of lost content, the happy going
and the happy ending. Roads remind us of the way we have
come and all the wrong turnings, the turnings to wrong and
all the waste: all the ways we might have loved as well as all
the ways we did love but not well enough. And because we

think that roads lead somewhere we expect life to lead somewhere, somewhere other than the grave. We are all born instinctive eschatologists, waiting, preparing for the thing, the success, the place of arrival, the person, the event, the sudden and final and complete stopping-place on the road that will be *It*.

But the credits can go up on the screen at any time: 'The End! That's it, folks. That was your life.' And you're still waiting for it to happen, still waiting for it to go somewhere, to make sense, to explain itself, to be resolved. Most people die as though a mistake were being made: 'Wait a minute, I haven't had my turn yet.' 'Mister, that was it.'

Mind you, it is not always as bleak as that. Most people appear not to think of these things at all. 'Humankind cannot bear very much reality.' There are all sorts of strategies, conscious and unconscious, for assuaging this strange sorrow that afflicts us, but they are all strategies of transcendence, intended, if they succeed, to distract the self from its own predicament.

There is, first of all, 'lateral transcendence', by which we escape, say, into work that fascinates us and engages our imagination. Work can be a very satisfactory substitute, for a time, for the longings that beset us. Work has its own eschatology. We can move through all the stages of success and achievement, allegories of the great advent which has been indefinitely postponed. You pay a price, of course, for this kind of transcendence, but many of those who pay it reckon it's worth it. But this kind of strategy of transcendence has only been available to a tiny fraction of all the men and women who have ever lived. For most people work is an unavoidable and stupefying necessity, not a way of transcendence: pick cotton, collect garbage, drive a truck, work on an assembly line or a check-out counter to find out.

A form of lateral transcendence that is available to more people is the family and the love it is supposed to enshrine. Even when we admit that the family is vulnerable,

19

particularly today, to all sorts of pressures that undermine it, it still provides many with a sufficient reason for living. There may even be some sort of inverse ratio at work here, which rewards those whose work is dull with an emotionally satisfying family life, while those with most job satisfaction have it rougher at home. That's only a sociological hunch. Certainly, the middle-class family, built uneasily around those two-career spouses, seems to be in all sorts of trouble today. However, families grow up and children move away and more and more couples seem to grow away from each other in the process. And there are always significant sections in our society that never make it into families. Nevertheless, the family, belonging somewhere, loving someone, is a way, for a time or half a time, of consolation.

Another route to lateral transcendence is through culture, high or low. Music takes us out of ourselves. So does sport, whether we participate or spectate. You can make your own list of diversions, some more enduring than others, whether they be nodding off to the music at Symphony Hall or damaging your eardrums at the local disco.

Other forms of transcendence are more problematic; 'downward transcendence', they are grudgingly called. Perhaps the most common, yet the most mysterious, is sex. If you exclude the frequently crushing physical pressure for simple relief, which can become compulsive and addictive, there is, behind every sexual encounter that is not violent or hate-filled, an attempt to break out of the self and its loneliness. D.H. Lawrence, who admittedly had a bit of a thing about it, maintained that sex was about gentleness; through it people try to comfort one another for their lostness and confusion. It is surely no accident that the sexual drive often becomes the focus and expression of unease and disorder in the self. The number of possible sexual deviations from the statistical norm is staggering and would be hilarious, if it didn't bring such pain and complexity into people's lives. 'Lay your sleeping head my love/Human on my faithless arm', sang W.H. Auden, and captured both the tenderness and the deceitfulness of human sexuality.

If our bodies often lead us on a sort of Pyrrhic search for transcendence through sex, various substances fill a similar role and usually claim an even more dreadful revenge. Alcohol and drug abuse is a depressingly familiar form of downward transcendence in our society. Drugs, even more than sex, fail to deliver what they promise, but it is the promise, in each case, that is significant. They are really displacements, forms of compensatory behaviour. We are really lusting and thirsting after something else, but these are to hand and the other thing is elusive and may not even exist, so we turn to them instead, and they cannot bear the weight of our longings.

Have we travelled in some kind of circle in this exploration, so far? We have seen the wayfarer, the migrant, the passing guest, as the Revised Standard Version translates it, making his troubled journey through time. Troubled, because certain mysterious pressures afflict him. Being human seems to bring with it a sense of demand, an inner disturbance that we resent a lot of the time. Our day is brief enough — why can we not be left to enjoy it before we depart hence and be no more seen? With the sense of demand comes a sense of resentment against this God we don't believe in, because he lays this guilt, this uneasiness upon us. Sometimes, however, the mood is not bitter, it's wistful, reproachful. 'Why lay your burning eyes on us, God? We're *dust*, remember? Quintessence of dust, troubled dust, but dust. Leave us alone. We don't amount to much. Please, look away from us, that we may enjoy our brief day.' Presumably God, or demand, or guilt, or whatever you call the troubler, presumably he does look away; from most of us, anyway. Some, however, seem to be afflicted with an overwhelming sense of whatever it is that afflicts us, and it burns up every other concern, including the most lovely and tender aspects of the earth's passing beauty. People like that, when we meet them, have some of

21

the same effect upon us that God seemed to have on the Psalmist. They disturb us. Something walks over our grave. When I meet them I sometimes want to slip away and cry, because I see something in their ravaged yet joyful faces that accuses me, accuses me sadly and tenderly but burningly, like the look Jesus gave Peter in the courtyard on the morning of his arrest. Remember that look? If you're not careful you can catch that look, be surprised by it, and you feel you've missed something in life. Missed the point. Missed an appointment you were meant to keep. As I say, some go that way, but most of us don't. God averts his gaze or we turn our back on him. However you put it, we concentrate on life, we seek to enjoy, like a hireling, our day.

Gradually a mysterious inversion takes place. There is much to enjoy in this heart-breaking beautiful world, much that gives us pleasure, whether it is the pleasure of sense or spirit. Increasingly, however, we are visited with a strange regret and dissatisfaction. We are not, somehow, experiencing what we are experiencing. The experiences won't hold up or won't hold us up. Bafflingly, they still draw us, still promise us something we think we're looking for, but something recedes from them as we embrace them. We become more and more aware that something is flying from us, yet we hunger increasingly for it. We fall into a regret that has something to do with the strange character of time and its sister, death, and its cousin, memory.

Of course, you don't have to get into all this. You can turn up the music and uncork the bottle and keep it all at arm's length — for a time. However, if you make the mistake of thinking about it, of brooding upon it, of tracing the theme in the broodings of others, you find yourself increasingly drawn into what Hopkins called a 'chief woe, a world-sorrow'. You realize that you are longing for something you have never known, you are remembering a place you have not heard. And somehow, everything is touched with the memory of it. The trace and perfume of it hang on everything, even your most satisfying loves, so that you become homesick when you're at home, lonely among friends, heart-hungry in the arms of the person who is filling your heart.

And then with the sorrow and the loss and the tear-pricking regret can come a sense of forgiveness and understanding, from somewhere. You get the sense, not of God's anger but of God's sorrow and pity: the divine pity! Something of it comes through the words of that sad and brilliant old sinner, Paul Tillich: 'you are accepted even though you are unacceptable.' So you think that maybe your flight wasn't necessary, after all. What is left then is not guilt or remorse so much as a tremendous sense of loss and waste. Do you remember the scene in Graham Greene's *The Power and the Glory* where the whiskey priest sits drinking brandy in his cell the night before his execution and thinks over his life? Tears pour down his face at the thought of going to God empty-handed, with nothing done at all. He feels, we are told, like someone who has 'missed happiness by seconds at an appointed place'.

Now, where does all this come from? Is there anything behind it all? Have we missed something? Is there a land of lost content somewhere that haunts us, though we've never been there? We know, do we not, that it is not the land of our own childhood, for we've been there, and magical as it might appear in retrospect, we know it was not particularly magical then. What is all this longing and harking back and looking up suddenly and recognizing heart-needs in faces we catch glimpses of in restaurants and on street corners, and in secret folds in the hill country, and in sudden stabs of music?

There seem to me to be only two brave and honest answers to that question. The first is the absurdist answer, which says Yes, we are tormented by longings and troubled by regret, but it all arises from nothing, nada, because, ultimately, that is all there is. It is an absurd, an idiotic universe, which, to echo C.S. Lewis, has produced creatures whose mere dreams are so much stronger, better, subtler than itself. In the words of one of the great and brave absurdists: 'Man is a useless passion. To get drunk in a bar by yourself or to be a ruler of the nations is equally pointless'[4] because there is nobody there! We are alone. Mind you, this doesn't mean we give up. Absurdity has its own ethics and its own prayer. The prayer comes from Hemingway: 'Our nada, which art in nada . . .'. And our ethic is an ethic of compassionate understanding, of forgiveness and love, for what else is possible as you look out on all those people you know, dying as they dream? It's the ethic of the *Titanic*, after all the lifeboats had left and it was just a question of waiting. An ethic for a titanic universe: basically, I suppose, a kind of wistful politeness; the salute of dying men to dying men. 'We must love one another before we die.'

The other answer I call the rational answer, though you may dispute the word. I call it rational because it looks for reasons, insists on answers, traces conclusions, because that is what human beings are best at doing. There is something in us that traces meanings, makes connections, finds out the mystery of things. We are not content till we have a working answer. So, the rational answer makes reply, all these strange promptings of regret, these longings and half-recognitions, point us beyond ourselves, beyond the earth. We are homesick because we are far from home!

Perhaps I can introduce what I want to say in conclusion by referring to a phenomenon remarked upon by poets and musicians. The Russian poet Osip Mandelstam, who was hounded to death by Stalin, wrote his poetry almost by dictation, according to his wife. It was a bit like trying to listen to London from America on a shortwave radio set. The voices come and go. He used to hear his poems coming through faintly, often at night, and he had to listen attentively to take them down. Edward Elgar is supposed to have said the same thing about music: 'Music is in the air — you simply take as much of it as you want.'

In other words, all this beauty that haunts us comes by revelation to those who are able to hear it. It is all around us, pressing in upon us, if only we could hear, if only we could learn to listen. And news of that other country we are born trying to remember comes the same way. We are homesick for something that lies beyond the universe yet strangely affects our world, the way the moon affects the movement of the sea. Our sense of regret points to a primordial homesickness — a sorrow that afflicts us precisely because we turn ourselves away from God who is the country we long for, the land of lost content. Most of us are mildly aware of this, but we are more than half afraid of the consequences of really finding God — 'Lest, having Him, we must have naught beside', in the words of Francis Thompson. The saints have a raging sense of their need for God. He is the country of their soul, and tidings from that far country break in upon them. That is the meaning of Christ, who brought tidings, news of that country. He brought the very air of it into our land of exile. And there have been other moments of revelation, brief glimpses beyond the curtain. The world rolls back, and we are left forlorn, but sustained by the memory of it and the sense we have that history, including our own private history, is the story of a return.

2. The Valley of Decision

In chapter one I tried to describe a mood that afflicts human beings. I called it regret, that mysterious sense of loss which overwhelms us from time to time. I say describe, but that is not the proper word; 'evoke' would be better. There are words and places and pieces of music that evoke this mood of regret, of longing for a lost content. Regret is a compound of many elements: the passing of time, expressed in the famous lines from Horace: *Eheu fugaces, Postume, Postume, Labuntur anni*: Years glide away and are lost to me, lost to me.[1] Death and all that going down into the grave is part of it, too. Autumn. Fall. 'Margaret are you grieving over Goldengrove unleaving?' And disappointment. With ourselves, with our lot. And a strange hungering in us for something we have not known yet feel, somehow, is our right, our destiny. We feel that we are banished from the land of lost content.

Now, we can do two things with that mood. We can use it to induce an attitude to life of compassionate pessimism or we can use it as the prelude to faith, the prelude to revelation. If we try to understand it, it can lead us to a state of expectation; in Newman's phrase, we are on tiptoe, looking for revelation, for the unveiling of meaning. Our sense of loss corresponds to reality, because we *have* lost something; our homesickness is real enough, because we *are* far from home. We have lost something that is not to be found in this life. We are spiritually displaced persons, seeking a homeland we have not known, yet are born remembering. This is all part of the paradox of regret. And the way back to the land of lost content is not by logic but by risk, by adventure, by romance. We have to go out, not knowing where we go. All the great quest stories are really parables of this great journey, the adventure of faith. The ingredients are always the same. It is the generous impulse, the risk, the plunge into the burning building or the fast-flowing river, that receives the great reward. Knowledge always succeeds upon faith, understanding follows commitment. We believe in order to know.

But once you enter upon this journey, certain problems beset you. Faith is a type of conflict, or it is a journey through many dangers, and, to a great extent, we travel in ignorance. After all, faith is not so much a method for receiving answers as a way of living with questions. Even so, we glimpse enough meaning to keep us going. The man of faith does not claim to know the answer to the riddle of the universe, but he discovers in it all sorts of hints and suggestions that point to an underlying purpose beneath the sheer and apparently senseless plenitude of being. He is aware of experiences in his own life where a tiny gesture has illuminated the whole meaning of his existence, and it is his own existence, after all, which he must make sense of. This personal responsibility for existence cannot await the unfolding of all mysteries, it must be tackled *now*. And it is his own private passion for purpose and direction in life that gives him the strongest hint as to the meaning of all things.

We ourselves are the strongest argument against our own doubts. We do not wait until the meaning of everything is made plain before doing anything. We operate on the basis of partial and fragmentary insights which give us enough light to go on for the moment. We live inductively, that is to say, we discover from our own partial experience and sense of purpose enough reason for living our own life, without being certain of the overall purpose of all things. If we are theoretically inclined, we may argue effectively from our own experience and the experience of others to a tentative general truth, but the general truth is a result of the private experience. There is no other way to live. It is impossible to live deductively, to wait until the total meaning is declared before embarking upon the adventure of living. That is to try to live life backwards, and it cannot be done. We move, if we move at all, from the meaning of our own life to the meaning of all life. No postponement is possible. We must read the meaning as we run. This is how we live, and it is the only way in which we can believe. The meaning of the whole is revealed through the part. We have no other way of knowing, we have no faculty large enough to absorb the meaning of the universe in its totality, but the totality can be mediated to us through the particular if we will wait upon it. When we humble ourselves beneath this necessity, we receive as a gift what we could not achieve by our own mental effort.

> To see a World in a Grain of Sand
>   and a Heaven in a Wild Flower
> Hold Infinity in the Palm of your hand
>   And Eternity in an hour.[2]

Next to the problem of life's meaning, the problem of suffering presses most painfully upon us. But there is something paradoxical about the problem of suffering, and we must understand it before venturing further. Suffering may be a problem for the believer, but it is a problem that arises *as a result of* faith and it cannot logically be used as an argument against it. A clumsy analogy from medicine might illustrate this. Let us suppose that I contract a deadly disease that will kill me unless it is checked and controlled by suitable treatment. The doctors put me on to a drug called 'X' which controls the disease and assures me of a normal life-span. Unfortunately, the drug has certain unpleasant and unavoidable side-effects which the doctors do not yet entirely understand, though they are constantly struggling with the problem. The drug impairs my eyesight and gives me periodic headaches. This life-giving medicine brings with it certain painful and unalterable disadvantages.

I can do either of two things: I can continue to take the drug and cope with the problems though I do not like or understand them. Or I can rail wildly against the drug and its manufacturers and their good faith in marketing it in the first place. I can give up the use of the drug. My vision improves and my headaches disappear, and in a few years I am dead.

We live in a mysterious universe. Belief in a good God lights up that mystery and gives it meaning. The fundamental problem of life's meaning is resolved by faith. But faith, in turn, gives rise to certain derivative problems, such as the problem of suffering. To give up faith because of the problems that derive from it is as foolish as giving up a life-giving medicine because of its unpleasant side-effects. In each case the avoidance of the problem only leads to death. The person who gives up belief in God because it brings with it certain unresolvable dilemmas ends up by believing in a dying universe in which there is no meaning anywhere, a universe that came from nothing and goes to nothing, a universe that is cruelly indifferent to all our needs. And there is no point in feeling resentment against such a universe, because in a godless universe there is no reason why anything should not happen, and there is no one to resent, no one to blame.

We are alone in an empty universe. No one is listening to our curses or our tears. We stand, tiny and solitary, in a corner of a vast and empty landscape, and if we listen, all we hear is the bitter echo of our own loneliness. The man of faith admits that his vision is blurred. He sees the mystery of life through a glass darkly, but he does discern some meaning, and one day, he believes, his eyes will be opened fully and all the painful mysteries of life will be made plain. The man of unbelief cannot accept this partial and faulty knowledge. He insists on seeing the plans and the maintenance manual for the whole of creation, and when it is not forthcoming he withdraws his co-operation. He rejects meaning. He breaks the glass. He is like a short-sighted man who plucks out his eyes rather than go through life wearing spectacles. At one stroke he crosses out the problem of suffering, but he only succeeds in leaving himself with the problem of life itself.

The sensitive unbeliever often feels an angry resentment as he contemplates the endless suffering of creation. His unbelief is a protest against a universe he sternly disapproves of. But this passionate resentment is itself a kind of faith. On one level it may not be very significant. There is a type of unbeliever who gives up belief because he wishes to punish God for the callous way he handles his creation. He rejects belief in God, but he has to bring him back in order to have an adequate object for his moral indignation. This type of rejection of God can be a real discipline that purges and cleanses the heart and fills it with an enormous pity for the wretched of the earth. Many of the secular saints of this century have been men and women of this mould who have given themselves to the services of their fellows, driven by an anguished love that finds no support from their own convictions about the ultimate structure of reality. Theirs is the heroism of despair. Though they may not themselves realize it, however, their own heroism and indignation provide fascinating clues to the very reality they deny. How can we account for their sense of moral outrage in a universe that is supposed to be massively indifferent to the sufferings of humanity? Whence do they derive the courage to love and serve, if the universe is ultimately hideous and unfeeling? How does pity emerge from this unechoing emptiness? These problems are as impressive as the problem of evil and suffering, though less spoken of. If we are to allow the problem of evil to state itself with such stark clarity, then we must allow the problem of good equal time in the debate. And goodness is as much a problem for the unbeliever as is evil for the believer. The data are every bit as impressive. History is filled with examples of heart-wrenching charity and self-sacrifice and nobility. The good have influenced men and women and their affairs quite as dramatically as have their villainous counterparts. Even in situations of the keenest misery and deprivation, human love and goodness have shone through with an unconquerable simplicity. Beneath the surface of the great tragedies and convulsions of history, people have loved and served each other with unregarded quietness. And even the sub-human creation reflects this same mystery: the care shown by all creatures for their young; the amazing heroism shown by the tiniest bird in following its strange migrant urge; and the marvellous spectacle of life itself in the ordering of the seasons and the grandeur of the earth. There is as much to lift the heart in the universe as there is to depress the mind; there is as much majesty as there is misery. Is there more logic in believing the worst possible than in believing the best possible? Faith, on the evidence, need not feel herself to be inadequately protected from the testimony of her accusers. It is not her task to make a case for herself, but when she is challenged to do so she is in just as strong a position as her more pessimistic sister.

> And now what are we? unbelievers both,
> Calm and complete, determinately fixed
> Today, tomorrow and for ever, pray?
> You'll guarantee me that? Not so, I think!
> In no wise! all we've gained is, that belief,
> As unbelief before, shakes us by fits,
> Confounds us like its predecessor. Where's
> The gain? how can we guard our unbelief,
> Make it bear fruit to us — the problem here.
> Just when we are safest, there's a sunset-touch,
> A fancy from a flower-bell, someone's death,
> A chorus-ending from Euripides, —
> And that's enough for fifty hopes and fears
> As old and new at once as nature's self,
> To rap and knock and enter in our soul,
> Take hands and dance there, a fantastic ring,
> Round the ancient idol, on his base again, —

The grand Perhaps! We look on helplessly.
There the old misgivings, crooked questions are —
This good God, — what he could do, if he would,
Would, if he could — then must have done long since:
If so, when, where and how? some way must be, —
Once feel about, and soon or late you hit
Some sense, in which it might be, after all.
Why not, 'The Way, the Truth, the Life'?[3]

Nevertheless, we must continue our enquiry, our exploration. What speculative answers have been given to the problem of suffering? How have the communities of faith accounted for it? Before we look at what is offered, we would do well to recall the epigram attributed to F.D. Maurice: 'Men are usually right in what they affirm and wrong in what they deny'. I take that to mean that there is usually some degree of truth in any serious answer that has been given to life's problems; so it behooves us to find the truth in answers that may, at first, appear to have little to offer. Well then, what answers are given to this great problem, what accounts are given? There are two interpretative myths that have emerged in religious thought to account for the great problems of suffering. We might call them the 'expulsion' and the 'search'.

It is hard to find the right word here, but the sense in millennia of religious meditation, fed by revelatory insight, is that the human predicament had its origin away back in some primal catastrophe, some fatal, false choice or act of rebellion, which led to an expulsion from the land of lost content. Some theologians have talked about a pre-cosmic fall. The very matter out of which creation as we know it evolved has been, somehow, vitiated, flawed from the very beginning. No matter how hard you try, it is impossible to get beyond some original contest of wills, some strike within the very enclosure of divinity.

There was war in heaven, Michael and his angels
fighting against the dragon; and the dragon and
his angels fought, but they were defeated and
there was no longer any place for them in heaven.
And the great dragon was thrown down, that
ancient serpent, who is called the Devil and Satan,
the deceiver of the whole world — he was thrown
down to earth, and his angels were thrown down
with him.

(Revelation 12.7-9)

What we are to understand here is that there has been
some sort of rebellion at the heart of reality, there has been
war in heaven, and it has been partly successful. The agents
of that rebellion have taken over and, to a great extent, still
control a part of the great empire. They are holding out in
one of the colonies. There is a *de facto* ruler of this world.
The words come from the New Testament, which describes
the devil as the 'ruler of the world'. 'And the devil took him
up, and showed him all the kingdoms of the world in a
moment of time, and said to him, "To you I will give all this
authority and their glory; for it has been delivered to me,
and I give it to whom I will" '. (Luke 4.5-6) Here, Satan
makes not only a usurper's claim, he makes a legal claim to
the world: 'it has been delivered unto me, and I give it to
whom I will'.

There has, apparently, been discord, rebellion in the
universe before us. There is some kind of civil war going on
and we are taking sides all our life. The story of Adam's fall
and expulsion from Eden, presupposes this earlier conflict,
for it is the serpent who tempts Eve:

Now the serpent was more subtle than any other
wild creature that the Lord God had made. He
said to the woman, 'Did God say, "You shall not
eat of any tree of the garden"?' And the woman
said to the serpent, 'We may eat of the fruit of the

33

trees of the garden; but God said, "You shall not eat of the fruit of the tree which is in the midst of the garden, neither shall you touch it, lest you die".' But the serpent said to the woman, 'You will not die. For God knows that when you eat of it your eyes will be opened and you will be like God, knowing good and evil'.

(Genesis 3.1-5)

The story of our first parents is, of course, our story. We co-operate, collaborate with the ruler of this world. In some mysterious but true sense, we choose against our own family, we commit spiritual and moral treason, we conspire against our own happiness, by siding with what we hate against what we love. Suicide, anorexia, addiction, self-destructive behaviour, self-neglect, child and parent abuse, predatory sexuality, anger, that mysterious resentment we retain almost exclusively for those to whom we are closely bonded, what are all these and many more besides, if they are not evidence of some kind of self-hypnosis that leads us to destroy our own happiness? And all this is in spite of ourselves! We get in our own way.

Now, however you lay all this out, whether in terms of rebellious spirits who seduce human beings into joining their own self-destructive revolt, or in terms of the historic sum of all free human choices for evil, the fact remains that there is a massive and deadening contagion of evil in the universe that bears down upon us all. And it is not simply a matter of consciousness. It has invaded the unconscious, even the collective or racial unconscious.

Surely some revelation is at hand;
Surely the Second Coming is at hand.
The Second Coming! Hardly are those words out
When a vast image out of *Spiritus Mundi*
Troubles my sight: somewhere in sands of the desert
A shape with lion body and the head of a man,

A gaze blank and pitiless as the sun,
Is moving its slow thighs, while all about it
Reel shadows of the indignant desert birds.
The darkness drops again; but now I know
That twenty centuries of stony sleep
Were vexed to nightmare by a rocking cradle,
And what rough beast, its hour come round at last,
Slouches towards Bethlehem to be born?[4]

It is like a vast and intricate fifth column that has moved into and taken control of almost every legitimate sphere of government in a state, and subtly manipulates it for its own ends. The result of it is that we don't know ourselves or where we live any more, because we have discovered that nothing is what it seems to be. We have not really been expelled from anywhere, but we are bewitched, so that home is foreign and friend is foe and foe is friend. Everything has been turned inside out and we don't recognize it any longer. That is why the novels of Charles Williams are so significant. He locates all these metaphysical battles, not in exotic planets in outer space, but in humdrum suburbs in outer London, where everything is ordinary to the casual eye, yet where struggles between good and evil are eternally waged. There is war in heaven, but heaven is all around us and the struggle is in our very midst, in your heart and mine. 'It feels like a war', said William James of the moral struggle. In war there is suffering, cruel, arbitrary suffering. We now, therefore, have sorrow and so does the sub-human creation. It writhes in travail, too.

Remember, 'Men are usually right in what they affirm'. This myth of struggle, of warfare between good and evil, has been around a long time and it corresponds to much of our own experience. Even the ancient understanding of suffering as punishment finds some sort of place here, for while we may dismiss that doctrine in its primitive version, it does contain a real truth: cosmic misery and human

35

suffering are somehow connected to a struggle in the universe that has its origin in a clash of wills between reality and the limits it sets, and created orders that have perceived those limits as some sort of challenge. Again, we get closer to this when we study it in our own hearts. I know that most of any suffering I have endured has been the consequence of my own rebellion against limits. Most of my suffering has been self-inflicted. I have cast myself out of the contented land.

If the myth of 'expulsion' corresponds to our personal and collective experience, so does the myth of 'search'. According to this attempt to explain the truth about the human predicament, human beings are not good things spoiled, seeking to be restored, but imperfect things in process of development. The land of lost content is not behind us but before us, drawing us forward. Our trouble is that we do not possess a really accurate map and the oral tradition, the tales we have been told about previous journeys towards the land we seek, tend to contradict or at least confuse each other. So we search rather wildly for what Tom Wolfe called the lost lane-end into heaven. From this perspective of the search the events we described as an expulsion are differently interpreted. The fall is really a step towards human freedom and responsibility and all its perils; it is a stage in our evolution as truly human beings. According to Eric Fromm, the thing that characterizes us as human is the freedom to create our own destiny. In the account given in Genesis, man is created in God's likeness with a capacity for evolution of which the limits are not set. 'God', says a Hasidic master, 'does not say that "it was good" after creating man; that indicates that while the cattle and everything else were finished after being created, man was not finished'. So we are given a role in our own creation, we are co-creators with God of our own destiny. We have been given the fateful gift of freedom. John Hick identifies this freedom with the fall. He says:

The creation of man in his own relatively autonomous world, in which he is cognitively free in
relation to his Maker, is what mythological
language calls the Fall of Man . . . Man exists at a
distance from God's goal for him, however, not
because he has fallen from that goal but because
he has yet to arrive at it.[5]

According to the myth of the 'search', sin is really a
missing of the mark due to ignorance and lack of skill,
rather than to premeditated malice. All the sufferings of
individuals and of the created order are the growing pains of
a universe still in process, seeking to find its own destiny.
God has created it free, in some sense, and, like any young
person, it runs inevitably into pain as it tests its own limits
and the limits of external reality. Suffering, therefore, is
like the travail of childbirth, or the pain of disciplined study
or athletic training: it is an inevitable concomitant of
growth. Moreover, we don't understand all of it. Some of it
seems meaningless, but it is all part of the travail and testing
of freedom. That expulsion from Eden is the necessary
preliminary to real maturity. Something of this comes
through in Milton's famous words:

> They looking back, all th'eastern side beheld
> Of Paradise, so late their happy seat,
> Wav'd over by that flaming brand, the Gate
> With dreadful faces throng'd and fiery arms.
> Some natural tears they dropped, but wiped them
>   soon;
> The world was all before them, where to choose
> Their place of rest, and Providence their guide:
> They, hand in hand, with wandering steps and slow
> Through Eden took their solitary way.[6]

So life on earth is a vale of soul-making, a valley of
decision, in which we are made or unmade as persons by the

way we have lived, the choices we have taken, the thing we have become.

> Multitudes, multitudes,
>   in the valley of decision!
> For the day of the Lord is near
>   in the valley of decision.
>   (Joel 3.14)

Now, there is clearly much truth in each of these myths (and we must remember that myths are not fictions; they are truths that transcend the merely factual). Each corresponds to real human experience. We feel ourselves caught in a strange paradox: fallen, lost, rebellious, sometimes hopeless; yet, at the same time, searching, struggling, discovering, growing. The misery and the majesty of man. There is an old Jewish saying about a man who carried two texts in his pockets, one telling him he was dust and ashes and the other that for him the whole world was made. Any balanced human religion or philosophy will affirm both. In theological categories, we need to be saved, rescued, redeemed; and we need to be sanctified, we need to grow and mature spiritually. We are justified by faith, because only God can save us; and by works, because he has given us a part to play.

Behind both myths there lies a single, surprising truth: God has limited himself with reference to his creation.

3. A Death in Jerusalem

I have called this part 'an exploration' because, in some sense, I am trying to journey into certain aspects of the Christian tradition. In a quite different sense, however, this chapter is exploratory because it ventures into more mysterious territory where the landmarks are strange and one walks with less confidence. In the first part of this exploration into suffering I talked about an experience I have lived with, as have many others. That was the experience of regret, and I tried to enter it, to discern where it comes from, where it leads to. Then I tried to talk about theories that attempt to explain or account for the problem of suffering in a chapter that looked at two of the ways in which people have accounted for the way things are. To a certain extent that was all in charted territory. I do not think there are any reliable maps for the territory I want to explore now. There are rumours and ideas in abundance, but there is no precise and detailed survey of the place. I want to look at some of these rumours and ideas. They have been lying around history, many of them, since men and women started thinking. I hope that by bringing them together a pattern may emerge, a meaning may be disclosed to us.

In one of his books Peter Berger quotes a story about a priest who lived a hidden life among the poor in a densely packed slum. No one came to the little room where he kept the Blessed Sacrament and said his prayers and celebrated Mass. There seemed to be no interest among his neighbours in what he stood for. He was an unseen Christian presence in the midst of a teeming, miserable, pain-ridden slum.

Someone asked him why he persisted, since he seemed to be getting nowhere. In reply, he said that he knew his ministry did not amount to much, but he carried on because he wanted to keep the rumour of God alive. That has always been a very evocative story for me. When we talk about the spiritual life we are dealing with rumours of mysterious realities that we can never quite pin down but that continue to haunt us: the meaning of life, the problem of pain, the mystery of suffering. History is full of rumours about these things, divine rumours, news of mysterious sightings, glimpses, sudden openings in the curtain that surrounds us. I'd like to listen to some of these rumours.

First of all, there is religion itself. In spite of the confident predictions of generations of sociologists, religion persists stubbornly in the human imagination, though it frequently takes on bizarre shapes. Most religions have certain common elements. Perhaps the most basic is the mysterious yearning for and identification of a reality that is not limited and confined to this world. Rumours of the existence of such a reality persist, and so does the strange power of sacred writings. The divine rumour is still discoverable in sacred scriptures in spite of the relentless efforts of academics to squeeze the magic from them. If we stop treating them like college text books, they still have power to scorch us with the intensity and cruelty of their vision. Where did it all come from? How did men and women manage to get this blazing, passionate, often rough and ugly information down in writing? Reading them, whether our own Christian scriptures or Hindu or Persian scriptures, gives one a sense of the enormous pressure of some kind of spiritual reality upon the lives of men and women of genius. A majestic rumour from somewhere has penetrated the minds of some of the most interesting characters in history.

And what about the experiences that have never been recorded: the ordinary, often puzzled revelations given to ordinary people, sudden glimpses into the meaning of things at odd moments, crossing a street, climbing a steep field to feed the sheep, on Hampstead Heath, 'sometimes at your prayers, sometimes hesitating at the angles of stairs', moments suddenly aglow with joy and a sense of the unity of all things.

What about poetry and music? Where do they come from? Was Elgar right when he said, 'Music is in the air — you simply take as much of it as you want'. Do music and poetry invade us from another type of reality that tries to get through and into our particular and limited reality?

Holiness has something of the same power as poetry and music, and I have often wondered where it comes from. I have known a handful of really holy people in my life, people who seemed transparent to the spiritual world. I do not mean they were moderately good and struggling, like most of us: rather, they were translucent. Though they were planted firmly enough in this world, an air from that other world came through them, a breath of the supernatural. Where does holiness, great sanctity, come from? There has never been a time without it, though some religious cultures produce more of it than others.

As impressive, in its own way, as sanctity is brilliance, genius, sheer human cleverness. Where does a single new idea come from? And think how many ideas there are, whole libraries full of them, explaining discoveries that have been made, connections that have been observed. Many of the really important discoveries seem to come in a strange kind of accidental, serendipitous moment of revelation: a brilliant mathematician is waiting for a 'bus and suddenly something pings into his mind, an unargued yet mysteriously self-evident conclusion. He dashes home and seeks to falsify the conclusion that has come to him and discovers that he cannot: a new scientific breakthrough has come by revelation.

What kind of universe is it that throws up religions and sacred scriptures, music and poetry, holiness and genius?

41

Naturalistic answers can be given to that question, but they don't seem to me to fit the strangeness of the universe. Others are free to choose that answer, if they please. I cannot, for long. It seems to me that to believe mere chance threw up Jesus Christ and Francis of Assisi and Samuel Johnson and Beethoven's Ninth Symphony and the Sistine Chapel and Dante's poetic vision is as convincing as claiming that if you left a chimpanzee long enough with a typewriter he would come up with the works of Shakespeare. The wild surmise of faith seems to me to fit the strangeness of the universe better than the cautious equations of disbelief. But faith only opens the door to more difficulties, though ten thousand difficulties do not make doubt. We suffer from two things: the problem of meaning, of trying to make sense of reality; and the problem of pain and suffering, of loss and regret. Faith makes the problem of meaning manageable, but it increases the problem of pain. If everything is ultimately meaningless, pain is not a problem, it's just an unpleasant fact. However, if you have resolved the problem of meaning by an act of faith that in some sense interprets and explains the universe, then it gives rise, by a secondary process, to the problem of pain. How do you fit pain into the assumption that there is meaning, that there is goodness and glory and joy enwrapping the universe? If faith enables us to live with the pain of the problem of meaning, how do we deal with the meaning of the problem of pain?

In the last chapter I looked at two explanatory myths, the myth of expulsion and the myth of search. They can both be put into a kind of syllogism. We are at war with reality. In war there is suffering. Therefore, we suffer. There *is* a sense in which we feel this to be true. We experience life as a struggle, something is awry, something has arisen, some treason at the heart of reality. The myth of the search looked at the same data from a different perspective. We are still growing into perfect maturity. There is unavoidable suffering in growing up. Therefore, we suffer. So we are afflicted by the pains of expulsion, rebellion, treason; or the pains of search, growth, the pangs of childbirth.

These are broad, interpretative myths that correspond to some extent with our experience, but they are theoretical, they do not really answer our hearts' needs. They are suggestive, they fit some of the facts, but they don't actually satisfy us. They reach our minds and trigger a vaguely affirming response, but we need much more than that. We need to be dragged out of our minds, we need to affirm with our whole being, offer our consent to something that will have to be vaster and more compelling than a syllogism, even though it is only glimpsed through a mist. Whatever meaning there is out there, it will have to come to us in flashes of metaphor, in the poetry of a human life. I want now to look at some of those metaphors, some of that poetry.

There is, for instance, the law of sacrifice. It is very easy for our modern consciousness to dismiss Old Testament descriptions of sacrifice, but at the heart of it there is something of profound importance going on, something mysteriously suggestive. We must not bring to a consideration of Old Testament sacrifice too many glib, modern presuppositions. If we do that we'll never really enter the truth of what is happening, we'll dismiss it all as a system of superstitious bribery of divine power. Certainly something like that may be going on in sacrifice. It may be that the original idea behind sacrifice is the placating or appeasing of a hostile power that is perceived as being superior to men and women and has a dangerous authority over them. This fearfulness is seen at its ultimate in human sacrifice, which is the final offering to this unseen yet powerfully arbitrary force behind existence. Yet even here we have to be careful. One of the most important texts on the subject is found in Genesis:

Every moving thing that lives shall be food for you; and as I gave you the green plants, I give you

43

everything. Only you shall not eat flesh with its life, that is, its blood.

(Gen. 9.3-4)

Apparently, the significance of sacrifice lies not in the death that is enacted but in the life that is released. We find the same theme in Leviticus:

> If any man of the house of Israel or of the strangers that sojourn among them eats any blood, I will set my face against that person who eats blood, and will cut him off from among his people. For the life of the flesh is in the blood: and I have given it for you upon the altar to make atonement for your souls; for it is the blood that makes atonement by reason of the life.

(Lev. 17.10-11)

So sacrifice is not about killing or ritual murder, it is about giving life back to God and the life is in the blood. That is why Jews do not eat the blood to this day. Sacrifice is about life, not death. Life is being returned to God and in order to release that life a death must be exacted, but the death is not the intention; it is, rather, the secondary effect. Sometimes in order to achieve one end you have to encompass another. Sometimes in order to save the life of a mother you have to abort a child, but your intention is not the destruction of the child, it is the saving of the mother. The destruction of the child is the tragic, secondary effect of your primary intention, which is the saving of the life of the mother. It could be that in the law of sacrifice and the primitive mind that lies behind it is this idea, not of giving a death to God but of giving a life to God, of affirming life. The secondary and unavoidable concomitant of this act is the destruction of a bullock or a goat or a girl from the village. Central to the idea of sacrifice, therefore, is the idea of return, of reattribution. The thing sacrificed or returned is the symbol or bearer of everything else. A sense comes through the system of sacrifice that we are not our own, that we belong to something else, and we are returning ourselves to it. This is the meaning of the tithe, of giving back a tenth to God; it is the meaning of the first sheaf at harvest; it is the meaning of the libation, or drink offering poured out to God. Inside the sacrificial system there is still something that answers to a question that comes from our own heart. The blood is the life, and the whole meaning of sacrifice is the return to God of the life that came from him in the first place. Beneath the clamour and the smell and the smoke, a truth is discerned: sacrifice is about life, not about death.

Related in some sense to the idea of sacrifice is the idea of vicarious suffering, or what Charles Williams called the law of exchange. There are two elements in the idea: the more sweeping is the idea that one's suffering can be used to bear the pains, sorrows, sins and infidelities of another; the other idea is more immediate and personal, it is the claim that one person can carry the pain of another almost as though it were a parcel that he agrees to carry for a while. The classic text, though it is shrouded in a sort of suggestive obscurity, is found in Leviticus:

> And when the high priest has made an end of atoning for the holy place and the tent of meeting and the altar, he shall present the live goat; and Aaron shall lay both his hands upon the head of the live goat, and confess over him all the iniquities of the people of Israel, and all their transgressions, all their sins; and he shall put them upon the head of the goat, and send him away into the wilderness by the hand of a man who is in readiness. The goat shall bear all their iniquities upon him to a solitary land; and he shall let the goat go in the wilderness.
>
> (Lev. 16.20-22)

Through this mysterious narrative there breathes the idea of vicarious suffering, represented by the defenceless goat that is led away into the wilderness, bearing the sins of the people of Israel. But there is plenty of support for the idea of vicarious suffering in actual human history. History is full of examples of suffering that had redemptive power, and it seems to me that much of it has been borne by women. Two images capture it for me: the picture of our Lady holding the broken body of Jesus in her arms after the deposition from the cross, the *pieta*; and the image of St Monica standing on the dock as her son sails away from her, bearing in her heart the pain of his confusion and searching. These are images of the pain that has characterized the estate of womanhood. 'Rachel weeping for her children'.

Intercession is an aspect of expression of vicarious suffering. 'Pray for me', we are asked, and we do. Someone we love is dying of cancer or has just been deserted by husband or wife or has a child who has got into some hideously tragic situation, and we suffer with them, we pray with them. We take it for granted, but intercession is another element in the mystery that surrounds us. Through it, for a time, we take upon ourselves another's burdens. We may not be able to rationalize it, offer an adequate explanation for the strange impulse we feel, but we follow our instinct and take the cancer or the attempted suicide and go to God with it, carrying it in our heart, speechless, inarticulate, but present before God on behalf of the ones we love. Just as mysterious is the sense of support people derive from it. They have told us how they felt held up by our prayers, surrounded by the ministry of our caring for them.

Related to all this is the experience of substitution, whereby men and women have, quite literally, given their lives for others. Fr Maximilian Kolbe is an obvious example of this ministry of substitution, in which he gave up his life to save a Jewish father from the gas chambers in Auschwitz. Many Americans feel that Martin Luther King's death was a substitutionary sacrifice, part of the mysterious law of exchange, whereby it is expedient that one man die for the people that the people perish not. And Mahatma Gandhi's death has the same quality. Both of these slayings were quixotic and meaningless on one level, but they are loaded with a sort of sacrificial resonance that goes on echoing through the years, long after their assassins' names have been forgotten. We cannot quantify the saving impact of these deaths, but we feel they are not meaningless. On the contrary, we feel that some great power is released through them. There is a sense in which these deaths can be interpreted as tragic and wasteful, yet in some other sense they have enriched us and continue to send waves of redemptive energy through the rest of time.

The doctrine of substitutionary love is put quite explicitly in the writings of Charles Williams, particularly in his novel *Descent into Hell*. Williams believed that men and women can bear one another's burdens. In the novel, Pauline tells Peter Stanhope she thinks she is going mad, because she has a trick, she said 'of meeting an exact likeness of myself in the street.' Stanhope tells her he will carry her fear, he will bear her burden for her. Pauline finally consents to this extraordinary invitation and that is the beginning of her deliverance.

Towards the end of the book she recognizes that Stanhope's gesture is, in fact, the central mystery of Christendom.

> The central mystery of Christendom, the terrible fundamental substitution on which so much learning had been spent and about which so much blood had been shed, showed not as a miraculous exception, but as the root of a universal rule . . . 'behold I show you a mystery', as supernatural as that Sacrifice, as natural as carrying a bag. She flexed her fingers by her side as if she thought of picking one up.[1]

Now, that may be dismissed as novelistic licence, but the doctrine was verified by Williams himself in his relations with others, and there is an example of it from the life of his friend C.S. Lewis. Walter Hooper tells us in his recent biography that Lewis told Neville Coghill that he had been allowed to bear his wife's pain.

These are all examples of what Williams called 'mutual coinherence'. We are members one of another, we co-inhere, and this underlying identification enables us to bear another's burden, to take on another's pain, however tentatively and incompletely. Our experience of the fact illuminates the mysterious claim made by Isaiah that God's servant '. . . has borne our griefs and carried our sorrow . . . upon him was the chastisement that made us whole, and with his stripes we are healed . . .' (Isaiah 53.4,5).

All these rumours and insights and themes and laws of mutuality gather into a particular pattern around the death of Christ. It is as though that death were a magnet to draw together the scattered fragments of human experience into a revelational unity. In my attempts to gather up the fragments I have scattered throughout these pages, I want to use a revealing insight set forth by Canon Vanstone in his profoundly meditated book, *The Stature of Waiting*.[2]

Part of the scandal of human suffering is caused by the apparent detachment of God. He does not appear to be interested in what is going on. Behind that sense there lies what is called the classical or static idea of God as 'the unmoved mover', defined by the Thirty-nine Articles of Religion as having neither 'body, parts nor passion'. So we end with a notion of God as a remote metaphysical idea, off somewhere, uninvolved in the pain and passion of our living. Gradually, a rebellion has crept in against this 'static' idea, but we may have created a trap for ourselves by our rebellion. We are an activist people in the West. We celebrate the supremacy of action over passion, of doing over suffering. We have canonized a male type of consciousness, an aggressive, moving, driving, building, doing type of consciousness. We are constantly on the move, driving through time, and history bears the smudge and imprint of our rough and hasty handling. So the idea of God as passive and static and uninvolved offends us. That is why we have made him over, in our own image, into an interventionist God, a God who liberates by his strong right arm, the God of the armies of Israel. But what if the thing we are meant to learn about God is that he is a waiting, suffering God who is acted upon rather than acts? Is there some truth here that we've lost? Are we so upset about suffering because we are so busy and activist and obsessed with solving problems that we have not waited long enough to expose ourselves to the scandalous truth about the meaning of suffering? Is suffering, submission to necessity, the carrier of redemption? And is redemption experienced *within* the suffering rather than in being rescued *from* the suffering? The word suffering is related to the word passion, which is related to the word patient. It suggests being acted upon, enduring rather than initiating. Vanstone talks about the person sick in bed as a good example of this helplessness. Something in us rebels against this passivity, but our rebellion may be blinding us to a truth about the nature of God and the nature of meaning. There is meaning in waiting, and we find it as a quiet but insistent theme in scripture.

'Peter, when you were young, you girded yourself and walked where you would; but when you are old, you will stretch out your hands, and another will gird you and carry you where you do not wish to go'.

(John 21.18)

I waited patiently for the Lord.

(Psalm 40.1)

> Wait for the Lord; be strong and let your heart
> take courage; yea, wait for the Lord.
>
> (Psalm 27.14)

All these blurred images come into strong focus when we turn to the death of Jesus. Vanstone describes a fascinating transition in Mark's gospel which highlights this. Mark's is a jerky gospel, full of verbs and sudden movements and 'straightways'. Jesus is always moving and doing. Then, two-thirds of the way through, we move from active verbs to passive verbs. When you get to the heart, the revelatory moment, the climax the gospel builds towards, Jesus stops acting and starts suffering. Mark seems to be saying that the great thing that happened through Jesus was achieved by passivity, not action. He submitted to necessity, he did not rebel against it.

The same theme is repeated in John, and here the focus is on a few simple words. John tells us in chapter 13 that when Judas left the upper room during the last supper, 'it was night'. Vanstone does not believe the words are accidental or inconsequential. In the same gospel our Lord had said: 'Work while it is yet day. The night cometh when no man can work'. John wants us to realize that our Lord had worked during the day and there came a point when work was no longer appropriate: 'and it was night'. Now he moved from action to passion, from work to waiting. At the climax of his ministry Jesus allows himself to be taken and acted upon. He accomplishes the work he was given to do by the sufficiency of suffering.

Let me try to gather all this together. I called this an exploration, and when you explore you frequently take wrong turnings, but in that death in Jerusalem there seems to be a gathering together of all the strange, disparate elements we have meditated on. First of all, there is the blood of sacrifice, the blood that is the life, the giving back of the life in the pouring out of the blood, allowing the life to be taken for redemptive purposes: that is a truth which is

50

repeated throughout religious history. Even modern, sophisticated Western Christians use the language of blood, though mostly, it must be admitted, when it has been set to music: 'Glory be to Jesus who in bitter pains, poured for me the lifeblood from his sacred veins'.

And tied to the shedding of blood is the idea of vicarious sacrifice. Someone else's death can redound to our benefit, can affect us redemptively. We can say that of many deaths, deaths that have sent an impact coursing through recorded time, an impulse of redemptive energy, but we say it supremely of that death in Jerusalem. This death above all deaths has universal meaning and impact. No one can adequately explain it or explain it away. Some people, because it is so powerful, have developed rather ugly theories to account for the power and working of it. However we put it, it has been felt that this blood has a strange, continuing power.

We looked at the power of intercession. Well, this death is heavy with the power of intercession. He prayed for his executioners. He interceded for sinners. He prayed and made arrangements for his own family during that dying. That death was wrapped round with intercession. He prayed from the Psalms while he hung there. Every one of the seven words from the cross was, in some sense, a prayer. So his death was a sustained act of intercession.

And the mysterious experience of exchange or substitution is illuminated by that death. We cannot, of course, be neat here; we dare not overdefine. However, we can say that the death of Jesus evokes all that mysterious tradition of substitutionary sacrifice, of mutual coinherence. If Fr Kolbe died for that one man, then this one man died in some sense for all of us. There is a universality about his death, which is only heightened by the anomalies and mysteries of the narrative. It happens, with inexplicable inevitability, and that is about all we can say of it.

And at the heart of it there is an enormous sense of patience, of a sort of strong, brooding wait upon God. It is

the waiting Vanstone wants us to savour, to meditate on, to
brood over. All the waitings we dismiss thoughtlessly:
waiting for the telephone to ring, waiting for that letter,
that report from the hospital, waiting from a bedside,
waiting for the moment that is either a turning back to life
or a settling deeper into death. Or there is the moment of
waiting for the curtain to rise. The wait for examination
results. We spend most of our lives waiting, yet we
scarcely spend a thought on the stature, the status of
waiting, the power of waiting. What can you do on a cross
except wait? You can't even wipe the sweat from your own
brow. You are more helpless there than in a hospital bed.
The passion of Jesus Christ is an exercise in passivity, in the
power of waiting. All this becomes even more powerful and
extraordinary when we link it to the great Pauline claim that
God was in Christ during it all, so that all this was
happening in the very heart of God. Is there something here
we have missed in our urgency, our desperation to clear the
problem of suffering up? Is it a mistake to think of suffering
as a problem, when it seems to be the mode of salvation, the
very medium of redemption, the nature of ultimate reality?
The meaning seems to lie in acceptance, rather than
rebellion. Redemption is not *from* but *within* suffering. It is
the joyful or half-joyful or merely rueful acceptance of what
cannot be altered. R.H. Benson captured the sense of it in
his last novel:

> '. . . it's quite plain, surely, that there is one class
> of persons on one side and another on the other.
> The one accepts what happens, so soon as it really
> has happened; and the other does not. The one
> knows that the past is inevitable, and the other is
> not sure. The one is not surprised at things, and
> therefore does not resent them; he is behind the
> scenes, so to speak, and understands what it is all
> about, even if he cannot quite make out the

details; and the other looks on from the stalls, and knows nothing except what he sees.'[3]

In that death in Jerusalem we are given a glimpse behind the scenes, and for all its poignancy it heartens and confirms us; it helps us to accept what happens. We know that in the mystery of suffering we have arrived at the heart of faith itself. Suffering and its endurance, minute after minute, when we are certain we can hang on no longer, when we have ceased to cut a brave figure, and are clinging nakedly to God alone, are a parable of the life of faith. A Jewish novelist has written: 'O God, if you do not exist what becomes of all the suffering?' The death of Jesus shows us that all the suffering is found in God's heart. Suffering is the manner of God's dealing with us. As things are in created history it is the terrible shadow of his love. For some reason, 'we can only be redeemed from fire by fire'.

That, of course, is a most unsatisfactory answer, in fact it is no answer at all. There is no *answer* to the problem of suffering, and there can be no answer for us on this side of eternity. A sufficient answer would require a minute recitation of all the facts of history and their connectedness, as well as a direct knowledge of the mind of God. Suffering will remain a tantalizing mystery and an enduring scandal to the passionate mind. There are no confident answers. Instead, we are given, if we can bear them, sudden glimpses of inarticulate meaning, brief hints of the pattern beneath the chaos. What we get is poetry, not philosophy; music, not metaphysics. And those who can receive it find they can live without answers, for their eyes have *seen* their salvation. You can tell who they are, because they laugh with those who laugh and weep with those who weep. You can also tell them by a kind of silence that pervades them and by their strong and grieving yet joyous compassion. They are the ones who have seen, though they can never tell what they have seen. That never matters, however, because those who suffer are not wanting words. It is silence they want and knowing in the silence. The sufferers are God's little ones, specially dear to him because of their pain, and they know the ones who know. They know them by their silence.

PART TWO

THE CHRISTIAN AND THE SEXUAL REVOLUTION

4.   What Is Sex For?

'I too am a man under authority' (Matt. 8.9). 'You were bought with a price' (1 Cor. 6.20). These two texts from the New Testament underline one of the central elements in the Christian faith. Christians are people who live under authority, under obedience. They have, of their own free will, chosen to surrender their lives to another's direction. The first text was spoken by a soldier, a man who recognized that Jesus, like himself, lived under orders. He came to do, not his own will, but the will of his father in heaven. And Paul, in the second text, approaches the same thing from a different angle, this time from the institution of slavery. A Christian was a slave of Christ. He had been bought with a price, and was no longer free to go his own way. So, in some sense we must try to discover, Christians are not their own; they are no longer free to live as they like. They are under authority. Like everyone else, of course, they are free to refuse to submit to this authority. They are not compelled to join up or sign on. However, if they do, they are no longer their own masters. They live under authority.

But what is the nature of this authority? How are we to describe it? There are two different Greek words for it in the New Testament, and they both help us to understand what it is we are talking about. The first word is *dunamis*, from which comes our word 'dynamite'. The central meaning of the word is 'power'. We talk about a dynamic person, someone who has immense personal authority and energy. The power of such people often attracts and overwhelms us. It draws from us something that wants to be led or directed. Often we are aimless, and a more powerful person than ourselves can lend direction and purpose to our lives, though this is not always a healthy thing. In the New Testament, however, the source and origin of all power is God. One reason we become pilgrims and searchers after God is because we all feel, in our often aimless and directionless lives, that in God there is an immense energy of love and joy and happiness which draws us to seek after it and find it. We can say that the power of God attracts us. Something in us is drawn towards this great centre of energy, though the attraction is often a strange combination of longing and fear. We feel claimed by it, fascinated, yet strangely appalled. So far, however, this attraction is vague and unspecific. Nevertheless, if the religious instinct is at all strong in us, we feel that the most important part of our lives' purpose is to seek out this power, find its face, trace its meaning, share its joy.

The second word for authority in the New Testament is more specific. It is *exousia*. This is the word used to describe specific authorities, such as a judge or a government official. Here, we are not concerned with the realm of personal authority or magnetism, but with the world of order or government structure. In an organized world there have to be authorities, people who have responsibilities for the sake of the common good, and we owe them obedience. If the traffic is to flow safely, we must obey the authoritative directions of the traffic policeman.

The New Testament is quite clear about this: God is the great and lovely mystery that attracts us by its beauty and power, but he is also a God of order. There is a governance in the universe, a way things are meant to run. The purpose of this order is our happiness, but it is order, nevertheless. We live under authority. The universe is not ours to play with or damage or destroy. God's children are not ours to exploit. We are not our own, even. There is a pattern, a structure to reality, a meaning in things. If we would find peace, we must find that pattern and follow it. If we would know the heart-wrenching beauty of God in all its power and glory, we must also learn that he lays specific demands upon us. We are under authority. We are not our own.

The catch is, of course, that we can't prove any of this, as a mathematician would prove it. And this brings me to the second major category in Christian thought. If authority is one of the central elements in the Christian faith, the other is revelation. How do I know I am under authority? By revelation. The Christian religion is not something thought up by men and women: it is something shown us, something revealed by heaven. As Paul says, 'it came by revelation', it was uncovered, exhibited to people who could not otherwise have found it out for themselves. 'The word became flesh', and we came to know what was not fully known before. Of course, you can reject this. You can say you do not believe such things. So be it. Find something else to live by, and good luck to you in your search. Christians, however, are those who have surrendered themselves to *this* claim. The depth of their surrender may vary and be, at times, uncertain. Their own obedience to it may be fitful and weak, but they have made the fundamental choice. This, for them henceforth, is what they have found to be the truth.

What they have committed themselves to has two aspects. There is what is called ortho*doxy*, or right thinking or knowledge. This covers all the knowledge that has been authoritatively revealed, what we call Christian doctrine. And note, again, that we cannot prove this in ways that would satisfy a research scientist in the laboratory. It was revealed, remember? I cannot prove the reality of the Trinity by reason, though I believe it is consistent with reason to believe it. The doctrine of the Trinity is what was revealed to us about the nature of God. We may be right in believing it, we may be wrong. What is undeniably right is that this is what *Christians* believe about God, because, they say, they have been shown it and have consented to the authority of the one who revealed it.

The second aspect of Christian truth is ortho*praxis*, which is right doing or right behaviour. Not only do Christians claim to have received a revelation of right knowledge, they claim, also, to have received a revelation of right behaviour, of conduct that is consistent with the nature of the God whom they have seen.

Certain things follow from all this, and they bring us back to where we started, back to authority. No one is compelled to be a Christian. It is a free act, something you consent to. But once you consent, you consent to its authoritative nature. There is a fundamental givenness about it. There is much that is debatable in the Christian Church; there is a lot of room for genuine difference of opinion and emphasis, but there is a fundamental, authoritative core that makes it what it is. This is what we call the official faith or standard of the Church, and it is not something that we can put to the vote. It is not ours to do that with. We cannot, for instance, decide to scrap the doctrine of the Trinity because people find it hard to believe. There is some room for interpreting what it means, of course, but the fundamental truth is not ours to tamper with. It is part of the definition of Christian faith, authoritatively revealed. Orthodoxy is the summary of the considered faith of the Christian Church. You are not free to make it what you want: you are only free to believe it or not. And it is the same with orthopraxis. For instance, the Christian faith teaches that every member of the human race is a child of God, so a Christian is not free to be a racist. Racism is a heresy, it is a denial of the true nature of God.

I have emphasized the authority of the Christian faith over us for reasons that will emerge as I proceed. Nevertheless, I am aware that authority is a very unpopular word today. Since this really is an important truth to grasp before we can proceed further in any theological direction, let me offer you a paraphrase. The word 'exploitation' is often used nowadays to describe a certain type of relation between men and women. When you exploit a woman, you use her to your own advantage or gratification. She is not treated as a person with a unique and sacred identity, but simply as a means to some purpose you have, whether it be domestic convenience or sexual gratification. The opposite of exploitation is reverence. When you show reverence to a woman, you allow her to reveal her nature to you in all its richness and need. She becomes, not a means to your gratification, but an end which has its own integrity and which you must respect. When a relationship of mutual reverence or respect is established, each discloses their inner nature to the other and the whole of life is enriched.

Now, this is a parable of the authority of the Christian revelation. It is the action of God as he shows himself to us, but it is an action that is vulnerable to our indifference and can be a victim of our exploitation. It is very easy to ignore its integrity, its intrinsic authority, its interior authenticity, just as we can ignore these things in another human being. When that happens we exploit the Christian faith, we do not reverence it. We must first allow it to *be* in its own right, before we can safely begin to relate to it. We must, in some sense, submit ourselves to its reality before it can be real for us. Unfortunately, this is very much the reverse of the modern way. We ask not, 'What does this mean?' but, 'What meaning can I find in this?' We ask not, 'What demands does this make upon me and the way I live?' but, 'What adjustments must I make to this in order to fit it into the way I live?' In this way we remove the intellectual and the ethical difficulties of the revelation, but we have done a very peculiar thing that, in the end, leaves us poorer than we were before. After all, Christianity is a voluntary relationship. We are free to refuse it, free to deny it is true, just as we can deny the overtures of a particular person who wishes to enter our life. What is perverse and finally self-defeating is to appear to accept it while we are,

61

in fact, simply exploiting it to our own advantage, by making ourselves the controlling authority in the situation. This destroys our integrity as well as the integrity of the revelation.

So far, then, I have tried to make the following points. The Christian faith claims to have received authoritatively from God a form of teaching, which we call doctrine, and a way of life, which we call holiness. Mysterious as it all is, if we submit reverently and obediently to it, instead of endlessly pursuing our own purposes, it opens up to us something incredibly powerful and beautiful.

The disadvantage in what I have said so far and in the way I have said it, is that it makes the Christian life sound like a package that you must take or leave. For some it is like that. They see the light, and they follow it with absolute simplicity. For most of us, alas, it is more like following a light that shines on a rocky and mountainous coastline: sometimes it shines bright and clear, and we press on and make progress; then we plunge down into a valley where we lose sight of it altogether and search vainly for it; then we catch sight of it again through a break in the rocks, and so on. In other words, the Christian faith and the Christian life are something whose lights and power we acknowledge and long to pursue with clarity and directness, but we often seem to lose sight of them and lose our way and circle backwards and make but little progress to the height on which they stand. And this stumbling and struggling is true in our search towards the truth as well as in our search for holiness of life.

Personally, this idea that the Christian life is a search does not trouble me, though I, too, often wish I were at journey's end. For me the Christian life is a way, a pilgrimage, a journey, a campaign, a search, a struggle — with all the exhilaration and sorrow, all the joy and despair that characterize such journeys. I know what Christian truth is, but I have not yet made it entirely my own; nevertheless, I struggle towards it through the strange

62

dazzling darkness of God's glory. I know what Christian holiness is, but I have not yet made it entirely my own; nevertheless, I struggle towards it through the complexities of my own nature and its needs. Do you see what I am trying to say? I am trying to present models of growth, not static, once-for-all, take-it-or-leave-it affairs. There are three great models of growth. The first is the model of personal development. We are called to grow from spiritual childishness to maturity. The second is the model of freedom. We are called to grow from bondage into liberty. The third is the model of health. We are called from sickness into health. We are children, called to the responsibilities of full maturity. We are prisoners, called to the insecurities of real liberty. We are invalids, called to take up our beds and walk.

Now, the trouble with much pulpit exhortation and ecclesiastical rhetoric is that it begins at the end and never gets back to the beginning. It tells you what a saint is like, often enough; it rarely helps you move from sinfulness to sanctity. This is because it assumes, in Augustine's words, that the Church is a museum of saints and not a school for sinners. It paints a wonderful picture of the heavenly city towards which we travel, it is less good at equipping us for the perils and difficulties of the journey. In some sense it actually assumes that Christians have already arrived, while most of us are still desperately plodding along the narrow way that leads to the city, with many a slip and slither and headlong tumble off the road. God wants us to be holy. We know that we want to be holy, too. But what a struggle it is to reach holiness, that surrender of ourselves, our souls and bodies to God. And nowhere is this more true than in the area of sexuality. The classic Christian teaching on sexuality often comes over as something that merely prohibits or denies or is worried to death. This is partly because sexuality is an enormously powerful force, and every sane culture in history has found it necessary to find some way of limiting its potential for destructiveness. All power is

63

dangerous and some means must always be found to limit and direct it and use it constructively. This is no less true of the power of sex. We know that sex can be an expression of the deepest tenderness and love; but it can also be used as an act of violence, contempt and hatred. It can be the sacramental expression of a love that is sworn and pledged, or it can be used as a way of finding temporary escape from the pain of loneliness and the hidden wounds in our nature. It can be a gift or a weapon. It is so holy that Paul uses it to describe the relationship between Christ and the Church; and it is so evil and destructive that Augustine was led to identify it as the root from which all sin is sprung.

The hope in the Christian life is that this great power in our lives can be brought into subjection to God; it can, maybe only gradually after much struggle, be brought under authority and may be used creatively for his purpose.

It is a melancholy fact that the traditional Christian attitude to sex usually came over as being prohibitory. It was largely a matter of what you should not do and with whom you should not do it. This was often backed up with false information, as, for instance, when adolescent boys were told that if they masturbated they would go blind. Sex research had not yet been invented. People did not talk about their sex lives, except in army barracks, locker rooms and confessionals.

If we would get away from the negative, prohibitory approach to sexuality we must ask, 'What is sex for?' 'What is it about?' I want to look at two answers to those aspects of sexuality that are quite obvious to even the most cursory beholder.

Sex is for procreation, says the first answer. This is clearly its biological meaning. It is nature's way of continuing the species. If the laws of nature are, in some wise, the laws of God, then we must conclude that the only allowable form of sexual activity is that which issues in children or intends to. If you accept this point of view, then you arrive at a very severe but very simple sexual ethic. It simply sweeps away every kind of sexual experience that is not intentionally procreative. Among the many things that it rejects are, of course, birth control methods that interfere with the processes of nature. The only method of birth control which is allowed is the use of the safe period, called the rhythm method. Clear and simple and straightforward as this approach appears to be, it is, in fact, not as clearcut as it appears. The very fact that it sanctions the rhythm method of birth control shows that it does admit occasions of intercourse that are not directly procreative. This, surely, destroys the basic argument, because it does admit the possibility of non-procreational sexuality. By the same token, it allows the infertile and the post-menopausal to engage in sexual activity because, while in these cases conception is not possible, it is not intentionally denied. I find this approach sophistical and not quite honest, though I cannot deny that it has an honourable tradition in Christianity and is still the official teaching of the Roman Catholic Church. For those who are able to receive it, it offers the advantage of a fairly simple solution to the many complexities of sexuality. It pays an enormous price, of course, for it runs counter to the universal experience of the race, for it is undoubtedly the case that human beings have, throughout history, engaged in sexual activity because it is pleasurable. We can always dismiss this, of course, by arguing that the pleasure of sex is simply an evolutionary incentive to maintain the species. If that were really the case, however, I feel that nature would have arrived at a simpler solution to the challenge of survival. Be that as it may, it is a fact that we are now in a completely new situation. A hundred years ago you could be quite certain that, large as families were, not every child survived. A kind of balance was achieved by multiple pregnancies, because only the fittest lived. Nowadays it is different. Most children survive, so we no longer rely on the brutality of disease to keep the population balanced. Another major fact of our era is the existence of birth control and family planning. Given, then, that the average family is planned, are we to assume that the endless sexual energy of human beings is, somehow, to be abrogated, because it is only the hangover of an evolutionary stage that we have long outgrown?

It is here that the second answer to the question comes. Sex is for fun, not just or even mainly for procreation, say the proponents of this point of view. Even in the rigorous days before scientific family planning, it was well known that sex was used as a pleasurable activity. Nowadays we can be liberated from the tyrannous biological determinism that previously haunted sexuality. We can now enjoy it without fear or anxiety, if we take the right precautions. We must admit that there is some truth in this point of view. It is found in the Bible, too. The Song of Solomon is a grand poetic celebration of erotic love, of the delight that sexual love can bring.

> Upon my bed by night
> I sought him whom my soul loves;
> I sought him, but found him not;
> I called him, but he gave no answer.
> 'I will rise now and go about the city,
> in the streets and in the squares;
> I will seek him whom my soul loves'.
> I sought him, but found him not.
> The watchmen found me,
> as they went about in the city.
> 'Have you seen him whom my soul loves?'
> Scarcely had I passed them,
> when I found him whom my soul loves.
> I held him, and would not let him go
> until I had brought him into my mother's house,
> and into the chamber of her that conceived me.
> I adjure you, O daughters of Jerusalem,
> by the gazelles or the hinds of the field,

that you stir not up nor awaken love
   until it please.

(Song of Solomon 3.1-5)

Christian poets and thinkers down the ages have refused to concede that sexual pleasure, erotic love, is simply an evolutionary carrot to ensure the survival of the species. It is, they say, a gift of God. It is an expression of the joy of God.

Robinson Jeffers celebrates it like this.

Is it not by his high superfluousness we know
Our God? For to equal a need
Is natural, animal, mineral: but to fling
Rainbows over the rain,
And beauty above the moon, and secret rainbows
On the domes of deep sea-shells,
And make the necessary embrace of breeding
Beautiful also as fire,
Not even the weeds to multiply without blossom
Nor the birds without music . . .
The extravagant kindness of God.[1]

So we need not apologize for the joy and pleasure of sex, while recognizing that it's not as simple as it sounds. Sex is not a straightforward outlet for pleasure, because human beings are not straightforward creatures. It seems to be a fact that where any pleasure is involved human beings soon get it out of proportion, and what was given as a joy soon, for some, becomes tyranny. Wine maketh glad the heart of man, but it also gives rise to one of the major sources of misery in our society. Every joy, every pleasure brings with it an awful shadow, and all of us some of the time and some of us all of the time find ourselves in that shadow. For some the pursuit of sexual pleasure becomes as destructive and unrelenting as is wine for the alcoholic. There is such a condition as erotomania, in which the victims are consumed with insatiable sexual longings. They pursue the fleeting pleasures of sex into the darkest corners of experience, haunting the sad places of the city, restlessly chasing a chimera called pleasure, led, often enough, into disease and self-loathing. And this is not all. There are forms of sexual pleasure that no society can tolerate, such as the extreme forms of sado-masochism. For some mysterious reason, some human beings are afflicted with psycho-sexual conditions that only find release in bizarre and complicated and often brutally demeaning scenarios. Some are only aroused by very young children. Some are only aroused by the brutalization of others. There is, for instance, a particular type of pornographic film available, called a snuff film, in which some helpless girl is raped then actually killed, while the film rolls. There are, apparently, some men who will pay large sums of money to see these films, which combine extremely sexual brutality with actual murder — nothing simulated. The pleasure is achieved only because the viewers know they are seeing the real thing.

It must be seen immediately, therefore, that pleasure alone does not afford us an adequate principle, since pleasure itself is a highly subjective thing, and it is not a thing that brings its own validation. Some pleasures we judge criminal. There are pleasures we cannot permit, because they are achieved at too terrible a price. How, then, are we to tell legitimate pleasure from sinful pleasure? Where do we draw the line? Where do we find the principle we need to guide us?

At the moment Christian thinking on this subject is caught between a rock and hard place. On the one hand we have a traditional approach to sexuality that is rigidly biological in its principle of validation. And on the other hand, we live in a culture that has frankly and blatantly adopted the pleasure principle as its guide. We live in an era when sex has been Hefnerized. It is one of the saddest facts of our day that Mr Hugh Hefner, founder of *Playboy* magazine, will probably be remembered as one of the most significant people of our time, since he was one of the presiding geniuses who initiated the sexual revolution. Gradually he pushed aside all the old inhibitions and taboos. One of the characteristics of the sexual revolution is its relentlessness and insatiability. It never has enough. We move from the acceptance of soft porn to hard porn. We move from simulated sexual encounters to actual sexual encounters on stage and screen. We have moved in the space of a few years from coy and oblique references to sex literature to a situation where no novel will sell, apparently, unless it is unremittingly and boringly specific in sexual descriptions. We have let the genie out of the bottle, and it is leading us a merry dance. It is doubly galling when we recognize that, for all the liberation language that is used to dress it up, the sexual revolution has been crassly commercial from the very beginning. Sex sells. In order to make a few rich, all of us have been subjected to the most effective piece of mass indoctrination in history. Two aspects of the commercialization of sex particularly sadden me.

The first is the way teenagers have been programmed and exploited by it. Enormous pressures are imposed upon young people today to become sexually active long before they are emotionally mature enough to handle it. Encouraging young people to be sexually active is as unwise and dangerous as allowing an unqualified person to pilot a jet plane. Our sexual energy is enormously complicated. It is deeply enmeshed with our emotional lives at the deepest level. Few young people are equipped to handle such power. Our culture deprives many young people of their own youth, by plunging them into an activity they are not mature enough to handle wisely — and all in the cause of sex as fun. It is fun, but it is dangerous, mysterious fun. Mary Calderone put it well when she said: 'The girl plays at sex, for which she is not ready, because fundamentally what she wants is love; and the boy plays at love, for which he is not ready, because what he wants is sex.'

The second aspect of our modern sexual culture that saddens me is its impact upon women. It demeans and exploits women in blatant ways. Most pornography, whether soft or hard, depersonalizes sex and reduces its participants to sexual objects. This has always been a tendency among men. Their very language betrays this. They reduce this most human encounter to something mechanical: a woman is 'a good lay' or one or two others things I would not express in print. In American teenage slang a girl's body is now marked out like a baseball field, so that you can measure your progress along it, for all the world as if she were not there. All that matters is going round the bases. These are blatant examples of exploitation. I think something subtler has also happened. The sexual revolution was orchestrated mainly by a few determined males, but they have succeeded in recruiting generations of women to go along with them, mistakenly believing that they were made more free by the process. The result is a society in which there is much more sex, but it means much less. Everyone is available for short engagements, brief encounters. Meanwhile, our long-term commitments are in trouble. We are, as a society, no longer able to keep our word, stick to our vows. Some of us find it impossible to make the vows, say the words at all. All we can sustain is a series of brief, terminable relationships. We suffer from commitment failure, relationship anxiety — but we don't have to work at it because society today is made in our own image. In many ways it is an ideal society for the male of the species, who has always been more sexually predatory, more frustrated by ties and bonds, than the female. Nowadays he does not have to bother with such things. He can be as superficial and unserious as he likes, exactly like the attractive superficiality of the Playboy stereotype. No wonder marriage is under threat, and more and more men are avoiding it. Why not roam the herd freely? Why not live out all the fantasies Mr Hefner has painted so glowingly? As a result, a lot of women in our society are being hurt.

70

Somehow what we have created does not really suit them, though they have been persuaded to go along with it.

It seems to me that these two naturalistic answers to our question are inadequate. The human experience of sex is more complex and mysterious than the procreational view allows. But if we switch to the pleasure principle alone we are even worse off. The need for pleasure, pursued for its own sake, seems to inflate and ramify in very dangerous directions. This, of course, was observed centuries ago. Moral philosophers have always known about what is called 'the paradox of hedonism'. Hedonism comes from the Greek word for pleasure. It has been observed that pleasure is a by-product of something else; if you pursue it for its own sake it eludes you. Like happiness, it visits you when you are concentrating on the something else, whether it is fly-fishing or someone you love. Pleasure alone does not afford us any kind of principle for evaluating our conduct. We must look elsewhere for that.

5. The Christian Answer

Neither procreation nor pleasure affords us a principle comprehensive enough to cover all the mysteries and intricacies of sexuality. But there is another answer to the questions, the answer that comes, broadly, from the Christian tradition. The Christian traces everything back to God. We find the perfect pattern of sexuality within the Godhead itself. God is relationship and unity. There is interpersonal relationship or intercourse in God. This is what the doctrine of the Trinity means: there is, though the metaphor is clumsy, family life within the Godhead. The life of God is characterized by a self-giving exchange. The mutual surrender and love of the members of the Trinity preserve the unity of the divine nature.

Now, it is our nature and destiny to be drawn to that same state. Ultimately, we are called to share in the divine nature, but even in this life we mirror and reflect it, often unconsciously. We seek that unity and relationship, that connectedness or wholeness, which is the life of God. Sexuality, in a mysterious way, is a figure or symbol of our ultimate destiny with God, because it is a search for the other. We feel that it is not good for us to be alone. We feel, in some way, mysteriously incomplete, so all our life is a searching for a remembered unity we may never yet have known. And sexuality is one of the modes of our search; it is both a parable and, in some sense, a realization of our need for unity and relatedness. For the Christian, therefore, there are two ingredients in sexual experience. One is clearly a participation in the joy of God. We need not be afraid to affirm and rejoice in the pleasure of our bodily nature, but we must remember that these pleasures are the outward and visible expressions of something much more important: they are the sign and seal of unity, relatedness, bondedness. For the Christian Church, sex is part of a covenant between two persons; it is a reflection or earthly representation of the covenant or marriage within the Godhead, and it is a reflection or earthly representation of the covenant or marriage between God and his people and Christ and his Church. Sex is the sacrament of unity. It is the outward and visible sign of that inward and spiritual surrender which is achieved in a true relationship.

Theoretically, human beings could achieve that level of surrender and commitment with more than one person. In fact, it does not work out like that, given our distracted and selfish nature. Giving yourself to one person is difficult enough, without entering into other relationships that will also tax our ability to give. Made as we are, to succeed in human relationships we need to concentrate; which is another way of saying we need to be faithful, if we are to realize the full potential of the covenant we have entered. I'll return to all this in a moment. Let me now turn to something else.

I have already pointed out that Christians try to live under the authority of a particular vision or revelation. They are not compelled to do this. The vision is there, and we are drawn to it and try to grow into it. We believe that it is a true vision, a vision of what is real. To conform to it, however slowly and painfully, we believe, is health-giving and satisfying, because it conforms us to reality. To run against the grain of reality makes us unhappy, because it distorts us, gets us out of tune with things. Now, the Christian vision of sexuality is extremely high and affirmative. When we reach the ideal at its highest representation in truly surrendered and covenanted love, we are mirroring the very life of God. When we decline from that standard, we are, even if unconsciously, going against the real grain of things and, in the long run, it tells on us.

Let me now try to draw some of these threads together. The source and origin of all things is a God in whom we are shown a pattern of covenanted love, in which there is an eternal rhythm of surrender and response, because it is love's nature to give, to give itself up, to spend itself. If we wanted to bring in oriental philosophy, we could talk about the male and female principle in the Godhead, the yin and yang. What we have, however we put it, is a pattern of eternal mutuality.

And this dynamic and unceasing love pours and expresses itself into the creation. It is the desire of God to make covenant with creation, with all created things, so that they might share the divine life. The Bible talks about this covenant as a marriage. God is married to Israel. But a pattern begins to assert itself: fidelity on the part of God, faithlessness on the part of Israel. This pattern of flight from the covenant is called adultery by God. We find it described with particular sternness in Jeremiah. Israel's sin is what we would call the worship of other gods. To the God of Israel it is adultery, harlotry:

> 'You have played the harlot with many lovers; and would you return to me? says the Lord. Lift up your eyes to the bare heights and see! By the wayside you have sat awaiting lovers like an Arab in the wilderness. You have polluted the land with your vile harlotry'.

> (Jeremiah 3.1-2)

Likewise, the children of God are called into covenanted relationships, called to pledge and bind themselves in marriage. And here the same pattern emerges. There seems to be something in us that pulls us away from the divine pattern of obedience to a covenant.

The symbol is continued in the New Testament. Christ

74

likened himself to a bride. And Paul talks about the importance of marriage, not because it is a natural institution, but because 'it is like unto the marriage between Christ and his Church'. Here, too, the pattern emerges. We resist the covenant. We find it difficult to be faithful to Christ.

So we find a strange paradox at work. The very spring and drive of our nature is in the direction of covenant, of finding unity in relationship. But there is another law at work within us that pulls us away from our true destiny, from the real joy that awaits us. It is the whole purpose of God, therefore, to draw us towards our true joy. He works upon us to deepen our faithfulness, our ability to commit ourselves. He wants us to learn how to choose and how to abide responsibly by our choices. But all the time something in us is pulling us away. This covenant struggle is true in every aspect of our lives, but it finds a particular focus and intensity in our sexual nature because, perhaps, it is here that we find the closest likeness to the nature of God. It is here, therefore, that the struggle is keenest.

All of this, therefore, issues in bonding or vowing or covenanting. There are two reasons for this. First of all, it is in the nature of true love to bind itself, to make an avowal or pledge. Strong, confident love does this: it pledges itself in an act of surrender and commitment. It wants the whole earth and heaven to hear and record its vows, its solemn pledge. Not because the law requires it, but because it is in the nature of love to pledge itself into a new unity. But the vow or bond has a secondary function. There is something in us that works against the covenant desire, the strong urge to pledge ourselves; there is an instinct in us to smash our dearly bought unities into fragments, so the pledge acts as a restraint upon our weakness. It gives us power when we are at our weakest. This is what G.K. Chesterton calls 'the law of the second wind'. In every human endeavour of any value and significance there comes a moment when we are tempted to desert because the first, fine, careless rapture has passed. It is here that faithfulness to the pledge carries us, till we get our second wind and go on again with restored enthusiasm — till the next challenge. Vows are important, because they help us in the dark corners and difficult places. Let me try to pull these claims into a single statement.

Full, bonded, faithful love is the image of the Trinity, and it is the desire of God for us in our sexual relations. This, at its highest, is the Christian ideal of sex, just as absolute charity is the Christian ideal of personal relationships. Neither ideal is easy to achieve, and will probably take a lifetime of struggle. It is not simply achieved by taking marriage vows and living in strictly legal faithfulness. It is a dynamic ideal that may take the whole of a married lifetime to achieve.

What, then, about the unmarried? Here I must speak more tentatively. The Bible offers us the sublime, maybe unachievable ideal — in this as in everything else — and the Church ratifies the ideal and only the ideal in its official proclamation. Nevertheless, we live in the real world and not some ideal world, and the Church has to deal with the world as it is, with all its complexity and failure and mystery. I would like to suggest a figure for your consideration, therefore, as a way of gaining some kind of perspective on this problem. In this figure we can, perhaps, measure the ideal content in diverse relationships and, to some extent, gauge or measure them by the high ideal. So then, think of sexuality as a continuum that stretches from the full, bonded solemnity of the absolute ideal right down to the most casual and thoughtless sexual encounter. It is easy to judge the extreme cases. It is easy to see what is furthest from the ideal. This, of course, is casual promiscuity. Maybe it should be the object of our compassion, since much of it is a flight from loneliness: 'any comfort serves in a whirlwind' in Hopkins' phrase. Nevertheless, the Church cannot affirm it, even though it recognizes that there is probably hidden within it somewhere a spark of the divine longing for unity and peace. Let's come further up the continuum. There are relationships that are far from the ideal that, nevertheless, have something of the ideal in them. Many love affairs are of this sort. There is a genuine, if disordered, love in them. A good example of this is found in one of Rose Macaulay's novels where she writes this of one of the characters:

> 'And then I thought how odd it was, all that love and joy and peace that flooded over me when I thought about him and how it all came from what was a deep meanness in our loves, for that is what adultery is, a meanness and a stealing, a taking away from someone what should be theirs, a great selfishness, and surrounded and guarded by lies lest it should be found out. And out of this meanness and this selfishness and this lying flow love and joy and peace, beyond anything that can be imagined. And this makes a discord in the mind, the happiness and the guilt and the remorse pulling in opposite ways so that the mind and soul are torn in two, and if it goes on for years and years the discord becomes permanent, so that it will never stop, and even if one goes on living after death there will still be this deep discord that nothing can heal, because of the great meanness and selfishness that caused such a deep joy. And there is no way out of this dilemma that I know'.[1]

Further up the continuum are those stable relationships between the unmarried, which have become such a feature of our society. Many of these reflect many aspects of the ideal. There is some level of commitment, though, as they say nowadays, it is open-ended, and I would have thought that was somewhat contradictory, since commitments are, in an important sense, closed things. Nevertheless, we can see in these relationships a real closeness to the ideal. We can affirm something of their nature, though we cannot put the Church's seal of full and final approval upon them.

Finally, what about stable and pledged homosexual relationships? Here again, I must repeat, I am suggesting a possible way of looking at a tangled situation. I am expressing my own approach, not making an official statement of the Church's approach. Here, too, I believe that we can affirm much. I am talking about committed relationships, not casual encounters. I think that there are several grounds for offering a measure of affirmation.

First of all, such relationships reflect something of the unitary and relational purpose of sexuality. On the continuum I spoke about, they partake of several of the ingredients of the ideal. And a second thought suggests itself. In this area we have to develop a sort of pastoral versatility, by which we measure small gains in growth and maturity. By this standard, I have known committed homosexual relationships that have had redemptive value, because they have rescued people from some of the sadness and danger of casual and meaningless promiscuity. I find it difficult to believe that God does not rejoice in such evidence of growth. He is, after all, nursing us all up to perfect self-giving maturity. The final thing I'd like to say about these relationships is that the sexual component is not the main thing, any more than it is in marriage. It is friendship and mutual support and self-giving love that validates them, as they validate all our relationships. Where these ingredients are present God's heart is surely rejoiced, for these reflect the mystery of his own nature.

If you accept this figure of the continuum, it allows us to celebrate the authoritative ideal in all its fullness, without departing from it as the Church's standard, while allowing us to affirm much that is good and redemptive in relationships that may not yet fully reflect the ideal itself. I am persuaded that we must in this, as in all things, affirm as much as we can in people, as they struggle towards maturity, without diminishing the brightness of the ideal that beckons us all. We are called to reflect in our lives the very life of God. Few in any generation achieve the completeness of that pattern of self-giving love, but it calls us to struggle towards it, through all the complexities and confusions of the day. It is the great city set on a hill that cannot be hid and it draws us all out of the darkness into its own marvellous light.

6. Putting Asunder

I have already pointed out that Christians are men and women under obedience. We have submitted to a vision or revelation, and we seek to follow it in our lives. I also tried to point out, however, that this obedience is not a static, straightforward thing like driving on the right, according to the highway code. There is a mystery, an elusiveness about it. It captures us, in some sense, but we spend the rest of our lives trying to learn obedience, trying to make it our own. And here an important distinction must be made. The Christian vision or revelation is not a law in the positive, legal sense. The highway code is a helpful example. We make laws about driving for our own safety. They are straightforward. If we break them we are punished for it. They are part of a sensible social contract that citizens have with one another. The Christian vision is not a law like that. It is not an arbitrary, if convenient way of arranging things. In some mysterious sense the Christian vision of law is trying to communicate the life of God to us. It says, 'This is reality, this is the way things are in the heart of God. Obedience to it is not, therefore, something imposed by sheer power. Obedience is the law of your own happiness; it is to conform yourself to reality. If you rebel against reality you punish yourself, because you violate the integrity of your own heart.' In some sense, therefore, the law of God, the Christian vision, is a bit like the laws of health. To live unwisely and gravely flout the laws of health is, ultimately, to rebel against your own well-being.

The problem is, of course, that there is something amiss with us. There is a profound irrationality in all of us so that, as Paul says in Romans, chapter 7: 'For I know that in me dwelleth no good thing: for to will is present with me; but how to perform that which is good I find not. For the good that I would I do not; but the evil which I would not, that I do'.

So, then, we consent to the vision of God with our heart. We desire unity, not dissension and strife. We long for peace, not conflict. We yearn after charity, not hatred. Yet how difficult it is to realize these goals! How very easy to slide into their opposites, often against our own deepest longing.

There is something else that we must take into consideration when we are wrestling with these things. Voltaire said that 'history never repeats itself; man always does'. We go on repeating the same old mistakes in our lives, but here something positive comes as well. God is not only God of the past. The Christian faith is not only about an original vision that was handed to us like a parcel that we must spend our lives trying to unwrap. God is also the God of the present and the future. He goes on showing us new things. As John says, he guides us into all the truth. Through the reason he has given us, he has disclosed to us more and more of the mysteries of nature. And by this same process he has disclosed, in recent years, many of the mysteries of our own human nature. This, too, is part of the revelation of God.

There are two elements to deal with, therefore: there is what we might call the changeless ideal of God, and there is the endlessly fluid reality of our own nature and its history. The story of our salvation is the attempt to conform the one to the other, the attempt to align our fickle, changeful nature with the eternal truth of God's longing for us. I want now to apply all this to the problem posed for Christians by relationships that break down, especially the bonded relationship of marriage. We know what God's vision is: it is relational unity, that endless surrender of the self to the self, and that endless gift of the other to the other, which is mirrored in the life of God. All of which appears to be

81

endlessly contradicted by our human experience, where we are always breaking apart, tearing asunder what has been slowly knit together.

Our Lord's teaching of the ideal is clear enough. God hates all the separations that disfigure our lives and cause such deep hurt and sadness. Marriage is a life long union, wrought by God and, Christ taught us, 'What God has joined together, let no man put asunder'. Marriage is the very image of the life of God. To destroy it is to do violence to the nature of God and his will for our peace. Here, anguish is piled upon anguish. Christians stand up in Church and pledge solemn vows to each other, 'to have and to hold, for better for worse, for richer for poorer, in sickness and in health, till death do us part'. And yet we find some of these unions, entered with the clear intention that they would last for life, breaking apart, usually to the great pain and anguish of the couple. It is wrong to suppose that divorces are easy, thoughtless, casual things. This may be so among a handful of immature film stars, but it is rarely the case in the real world. Divorce is always terrible in the shame and pain and deep sense of failure that it brings. Everything I've read about it and all the people I've spoken to about it liken it to death, only worse, because it is a lingering thing. And, in one important sense, it never really takes place at all. This is especially so where there are children whom both parents love. This is why one psychiatrist has described divorce as marriage carried on by other means, with a bond of hostility replacing the erotic bond.

In addition to the anguish felt by the couple, there is the deep anguish felt by the Church. The Church witnesses and solemnizes the vows made by the couple, and now it is witnessing a wholesale destruction of covenants it solemnly ratified. The statistics are dramatic enough. In Massachusetts more than half the marriages that are ratified end in divorce. For the USA as a whole it is more than one-third. The average length of a marriage in the USA is now six and a half years. Children are showing increasing resilience in this situation, but surveys show that they hate it and are usually the ones who are most hurt by it. Children usually assume that they are somehow responsible for their parents' divorce. Many of them are caught in a loving tug of war over custody and visitation rights. There is no more poignant figure in our society than the weekend Dad, trying to squeeze all his love into these awkward and often uneasy interludes when he has access to the children he'd die for. A recent book captures all of this, *Marriage, Love, Sex and Divorce*, by Jonathan Gathorne-Hardy.[1] He eloquently describes the predicament we are in in a survey that ranges over every aspect of human sexuality, and he even manages an optimistic conclusion, though his approach is one that a Christian should interpret with a certain critical reserve. What are we to make of this? There are several elements in the situation. There are several factors that seem to contribute to divorce, although it is not wise to generalize too wildly. I would like to look at three elements that create significant strain in modern marriages.

The first is the myth of romantic love. There is something rather mysterious about being in love. The thing that characterizes it is the absolute idealization of the beloved, and herein lies its greatest danger. No one is ideal. When we are in love we tend to project onto the beloved a whole complex of needs and longings. In fact, we create an ideal that does not exist. There is little harm in this if there are other elements in the relationship. If, however, it is based on a false idealization, then disaster lies ahead, because romantic love of this sort does not persist for very long. If you like, it is the initial surge of power that gets us into orbit, but we need something much more reliable and consistent to keep us moving once we're up there. The Greeks have several words for love: *eros* is the kind of thing I've been talking about, that intense, electric and over-whelming fascination another person has for us. It is obviously related to our sexual nature. But there is another

Greek word for love, *agape*, for they recognized that real love is a disciplined and consistent going out towards the other. This kind of love is located in the will, and that is where marriages find the energy to endure. We live in a culture that has somehow contrived to persuade people that being in love is the absolutely essential predisposing factor in marriage. Most romantic novels end at this point, just when real living is beginning. It is a well-known fact that marriages between young people in love in this conventional way often end in divorce. The surveys show something of an exact ratio here. The younger you are when you marry, the more chance you'll divorce. The older you are, the more chance you'll stay married. You need something more durable than romantic love to endure marriage.

The second element, though I'm not sure how much weight to put upon it, is the contagious nature of marital breakdown in society. Inevitably, as more and more people become divorced, the divorced state becomes socially normative and people who remain married begin to wonder if something is wrong with them. This is not as bizarre as it sounds. I have read about certain communities where marriage is considered so passé that happily married couples begin to feel embarrassed. There is a sort of reverse stigma operating, and you have what commentators are describing as 'closet marriages', where the couple are afraid to admit to their condition. Those, I am sure, are extreme cases. Nevertheless, there is a contagious element in the current situation. As more and more people in your circle break up you begin to look anxiously at your own marriage. This is the theme of a number of recent films, a telltale sign that there is a kind of psychic infection abroad. Related to this, of course, is the ease with which divorce can be gained today. There are gains and losses in easy divorce, but one of the disadvantages is that it can lead to haste in a situation where time ought to be taken. This may be one reason why a lot of divorced people later remarry each other.

But by far the most important element in marriage breakdown, indeed in all relational difficulties, is the continuing impact and effect of our original family history and childhood experience. Sociologists call this, in their inelegant but effective jargon, 'the transgenerational transmission of family problems'. So, for instance, you ask the question: Why have these two mature people, who have sworn solemn promises to each other, which they sincerely meant, not been able to stay together? And the answer is that there were significant subconscious factors at work, which, in many cases, denied the reality of the marriage from the very beginning. One of the great new fields of knowledge that have opened before us in the last fifty years is precisely in this hitherto unexplored territory. We do not come into our relationships as straightforward, blank personalities, but as the bearers of all sorts of psychological freight. Often the freight we bear, the load we carry, the hidden agenda that lies within us, are so complex and potent that they make it impossible for us to develop enduring relationships, or relationships with particular kinds of people. Conversely, they may lead us into specific types of relationships that replicate the past, such as the man who wants his mother all over again, or the woman who wants to play the role of daddy's beautiful little girl all through life and picks a man who will play to that role. In the same way, many of the conflicts that appear in marriage have their roots in the families we come from, sometimes quite paradoxically. Children who were battered brutally as babies swear as adults that they will never do it to their children, yet research shows that battered children usually have parents who were themselves battered as children. 'History never repeats itself; man always does'. Many of the problems that beset us are transmitted to us by circumstances over which we have little control.

So it is fatal to enter into serious and permanent relationships, especially in marriage, unless we are prepared to discover and face aspects of ourselves that we may have hidden from for years. The really hopeful thing is that we are not imprisoned by our past once we have honestly faced it. When we know why we are the way we are; when we know why we react the way we do, sometimes disproportionately, sometimes with a sort of disconnected hostility; when we are prepared to work through some aspects of our nature, some elements in our family history that we have studiously ignored, then new life is possible. This exactly mirrors our experience of the forgiveness of Christ. Nothing can separate us from the love of Christ, except one thing — a dishonest perception of ourselves. But when we face all the truth about ourselves, hiding nothing, abandoning all pretence, then he takes us by the hand and leads us on again to that original vision that drew us in the first place.

In the face of the situation created by divorce the churches are having to develop new pastoral approaches. The Roman Catholic Church is an interesting case in point. There is no remarriage after divorce in that Church, but they have developed a flexible annulment procedure that is sensitive to the complexities of human relationships, without abandoning the doctrine of marriage as a lifelong union, broken only by death. The single ground for marriage annulment that has been universally accepted is that of physical non-consummation. The solemn pledge till death, taken in the exchange of vows, is not held to be binding in that case because, it is argued, the marriage never came into full existence in the first place. This exception modifies the absolute nature of the vow 'till death do us part', thereby acknowledging that the vow can be nullified by subsequent events. The idea of non-consummation has been widened. It is recognized that some people are not capable of spiritual or psychological consummation of the married relationship, so the marriage is annulled on the grounds that it was never fully realized. Achieving an annulment is a costly and time-consuming process, but the method, however cynically viewed by some, does preserve the Christian witness to the solemnity of the marriage vow, and it neatly side steps the anomaly of taking vows of life-long fidelity to a new spouse while a previous spouse is still alive. However, it involves the use of a legal machine that can be manipulated in various ways, and it gives to tribunals the power to pronounce absolute verdicts on the status of marriages on the basis of highly complex psychological evidence.

Churches that do not have the juridical resources of Rome have adopted other approaches, but all have major disadvantages. Many churches, for instance, permit ministers to remarry divorced people if they are satisfied that the couple really intend to keep their new vows and are suitable penitent about their failure to keep the old ones. This does nothing to remove the anomaly of repeating life-long vows to more than one partner, but churches that follow this practice usually argue that mercy, not law, should be the primary element in the Church's dealing with sinful human beings. They fully accept all the complexities and ambiguities of ministering to the divorced. The Church has learned to develop a moral casuistry in other areas, such as its justification for the use of force in some circumstances, following the doctrine of the lesser of two evils, so why will it not allow the same flexibility in dealing with marital breakdown? For these reasons the American and Canadian branches of the Anglican Communion permit the remarriage of the divorced, but the results are disquieting. Karl Popper warned us about the unintentional social consequences of intentional social acts. I suspect that one of the consequences of the new rules in the American Church, combined with the divorce mentality in the culture as a whole, has been the removal of the final defensive perimeter round the institution of marriage as a lifelong union. When divorce was socially and ecclesiastically unthinkable, marriage was endured, in some cases, long beyond the point of reason. But the pain that was endured by some chronically unhappy couples was compensated for by many others who weathered difficulties that in divorcing cultures would have blown them apart. A reverse effect is clearly discernible in America today, even in the churches. It is particularly discernible among the clergy, who are no longer professionally damaged by divorce and remarriage. One of the consequences of the new rules has been a dismaying increase in divorce among clergy, including bishops, and a dramatic decline in sexual discipline. A reform that was intended to assist the Church in its ministry to the divorced may be having the paradoxical effect of weakening the institution of marriage itself.

It is for this reason that many people, divorced people among them, favour the simpler method of a civil marriage followed by a church blessing, for the divorced. This solution leaves open the question of the ontological status of the previous vow, but it has the merit of leaving the decision to remarry and its consequences to the consciences of the couple. The Church declines to hear a second vow but neither does it pronounce officiously upon the present status of the first. The advantage of this type of creative ambiguity is that it leaves the question open since no one has so far produced a universally acceptable answer, while maintaining a strong and continuing pastoral commitment to those who are caught in the predicament of divorce.

Almost anything the Church does in this situation is fraught with difficulty. Christians are and will remain in notorious disagreement with one another over it. The parallel with pacifism is suggestive. There have always been groups of passionate rigorists within the Church who have argued that violence is radically inconsistent with our Lord's words and clear example. So far most people would agree with them, yet the Church does not say that pacifism is the only allowable norm for Christians, though it has never forbidden it to individuals. The argument has usually hinged on a sort of moral calculus that measures consequences as well as ideals. The paradox of pacifism has always been that, applied literally and universally by the good in the face of the evil, it can lead to an increase in the very violence it seeks to eschew, by allowing tyrannous evil to prevail. This has led to the doctrine of the lesser evil, whereby men and women in sorrow rather than anger will take up arms against an aggressor in order to minimize the violence and evil that might otherwise be done. One of the irresolvable disputes of history is the extent to which pacifism has actually contributed to the wars it has sought to avoid by setting its leaders naked before their enemies. No one argues that violence is ever less than painful to the mind of Christ, but Christians have to make broad moral calculations, remembering that the best is often the enemy of the good. The best is rarely attainable by us, but sometimes we can clumsily snatch a kind of good out of the situation by defeating the greater evil. That, in its way, is a kind of victory.

The Church is mired inescapably in history, ministering to flawed and confused men and women. We are all compromised. Imperfect ourselves, we must somehow witness to the vision of Christian perfection held before us in the Gospel. Maybe we hold so passionately to the Christian standard of marriage because we have compromised so hopelessly on everything else; but it does seem inconsistent to temper the raw idealism of the Sermon on the Mount to the realities of our situation in everything except marriage discipline. Maybe we are moving into a kind of moral pluralism that will permit a variety of styles in sexual attitudes among Christians, just as it presently permits a number of different economic attitudes, from the radical Christian socialist who seeks to topple the capitalist system right up to the conservative Christian principles. The rightness and wrongness of all these disputes can only be resolved eschatologically, after all. If God *is* operating an intricate moral and legal system in which there really are discernible rights and wrongs of an absolute nature confronting us, and if each choice we make is fateful and will one day meets its due reward or punishment, can't we leave some questions till judgement day? If God is really intent upon punishing those who adulterously remarry, then presumably what we do or don't do about the situation won't make much difference, except that it might offer some temporal comfort to the poor victims who have incurred the wrath of God. I am always haunted by Laertes' words to the priest in *Hamlet* who refused Ophelia full Christian burial: 'I tell thee, churlish priest, a ministering angel shall my sister be, when thou liest howling'. The Church has too often presumed upon its knowledge of the mind of God and turned a harsh face to his children in his name. Maybe God does not want us to be administering a legal system so much as ministering to the system's victims. Maybe we should recognize that the Church of Christ, 'that wonderful and sacred mystery', is caught in the strange dilemma of the chaplain to the whorehouse. For some the solution is obvious: you withhold communion till the girls clean up their act. For others it is more complicated: the very predicament in which they find themselves means that the girls have the greater need of sacramental grace and comfort. That's the dilemma that divides Christians, prophets from priests, the severe from the merciful. Christ was both; most of us seem to fall on one side or the other. But since there are certain situations in which we must choose the Christ we would follow, I choose mercy. I say, let them marry.

PART THREE

PRIEST TO THE WORLD

7. Looking Towards Jesus

Towards the end of the last century there was a movement among German theologians called 'the quest for the historical Jesus'. The men on the quest were very radical in their approach to the New Testament. They claimed that the portrait of Christ in the gospels was not historical. It was overlaid with all sorts of embellishments that turned Jesus into a supernatural visitant from on high, when he was only a man. What was needed was to cut through all that later development and find the simple Jesus of history as he really was. This was 'the quest for the historical Jesus'. George Tyrrell in writing about this group of scholars produced an epigram famous in theological circles. Speaking specifically of the work of one of the scholars on the quest he wrote: 'The Christ that Harnack sees, looking back through nineteen centuries of Catholic darkness, is only the reflection of a Liberal Protestant face, seen at the bottom of a deep well'.[1]

This tendency to project oneself onto Jesus is not confined to nineteenth-century Germans. We all do it. The tendency is almost inescapable. Jesus is seen as someone who reflects and validates our opinions and preoccupations. Parson Thwackum in *Tom Jones* perfectly reflects this automatic egotism: 'When I mention religion I mean the Christian religion; and not only the Christian religion, but the Protestant religion; and not only the Protestant religion, but the Church of England'.

This tendency to see in Jesus the validation of our

standards is not necessarily a bad thing. There is some good in all of us and in our opinions. Jesus affirms what is good in us. Sometimes he has to be seen as fulfilling and representing and in some sense consecrating our sincere convictions. The trouble, of course, is that we tend to stop there: we simply use Jesus to anoint our partial and limited point of view. We are not really seeing him: we are only seeing ourselves reflected in him. And this is exactly what most of the men and women of Jesus' day did. In Mark's Gospel Jesus asks his disciples: 'Who do men say that I am?' The popular estimates of Jesus, that he was John the Baptist come back to life, that he was Elijah or another of the old prophets, may appear puzzling, but they all fit into the predictable pattern of Jewish expectation. Their own history had imbued in them a longing for a heavenly deliverer. He would combine all the attributes of the three great figures in Hebrew history: prophet, priest and king. Since all these three received their office by a rite of anointing with oil, the figure they were looking for came to be known as 'the Anointed One', the Messiah, or, in Greek, 'the Christ'. Certain signs would accompany his appearing. For instance, some of the great prophetic figures of the past would reappear. 'Behold, I send my messenger to prepare the way before me, and the Lord whom you seek will suddenly come to his temple; the messenger of the covenant in whom you delight, behold, he is coming, says the Lord of hosts. But who can endure the day of his coming, and who can stand when he appears?' (Mal. 3.1-2). 'Behold, I will send you Elijah the prophet before the great and terrible day of the Lord comes. And he will turn the hearts of fathers to their children and the hearts of children to their fathers, lest I come and smite the land with a curse' (Mal. 4.5-6).

Then arose John the Baptist, preparing the way for the Anointed One. The people recognized him and so did Jesus: '*This* is Elijah'. He was part of their general expectation. He came out of their history. He was a revisiting of their past. He was not anything new. He was a gathering up of all that human longing into a great cry. He was a voice crying in the wilderness of the human heart, beseeching God to break the imprisoning mould of human history and do a new thing. But they identified Jesus with that past and its longing and expectations, too. He also was a rerun of an old film. They looked at Jesus and all they saw was a flickering projection of their own expectations. 'Who do men say that I am?' He was John the Baptist again, the superstitious said. He was Elijah himself, or one of the old prophets. He came from the anguish of their own past. That was the popular estimate. 'But you who have been with me, who do you say I am?' Peter answered him, 'You are the Christ'. In a flash of inspiration Peter recognizes him as the new thing they long for: the one from God with a new revelation, with good *news*, not simply a rehash of old history. At last a new thing had happened. A leap from the imprisoning system of the past. God had done a new thing. He had revealed himself. Only a few recognized him, and very soon the past overpowered their thinking and dragged them back to prison, because when Jesus began to teach them the awful lesson that all their expectations were wrong about the Anointed One and that he must suffer and be rejected, Peter rebuked him: 'You've got it wrong, master. That's not what the book says. You are supposed to rule, not suffer; you are supposed to have universal acclaim, not be rejected. Even though you are the Christ, you've got to be the Christ we want, the one we've been banking on. You've got to be an expression of our longing, a projection of our needs. You've got to be what we want'. Jesus, we read, sternly rebuked Peter: 'Get behind me, Satan'. But, if Jesus wasn't just another man from the tired old past, what was he? Before attempting to answer that, let me say, first, why the answer is important.

We miss something terribly important if we continue to use Jesus as some kind of projection of or sanction for our own aspirations and opinions. When we do that we are simply locking ourselves into ourselves, we are not letting him work on us in ways that might transform us. Somehow, we have to learn to start looking at Jesus and let him be himself, no matter how disturbing that might be. We have to try to hear *him*, and not just the echo of our own voice. If we do this long enough, then something new can start in us. He can slowly transform us, draw us out of ourselves. As the psalm says, 'he can lift us like a bird out of the snare of the fowler'.

How, then, are we to think about Jesus and the conviction Christians have about him?

Think of it as a man in a chariot being pulled by a powerful horse. The man has two reins in his hands. If he holds them both, the horse will pull him forward. If he drops one rein, then he'll simply go round in a circle. Now, the New Testament is quite clear about one thing: it is *Christ* who is the central fact of the Christian faith. But there is something paradoxical about Christ, two apparently contradictory things have to be held together, like the reins on a horse: drop one of them and you make no progress.

First of all, then, the New Testament is quite clear about the *humanity* of Jesus. The Letter to the Hebrews is a representative witness. 'Jesus had to be made like his brethren in every respect, so that he might become a merciful and faithful high priest in the service of God, to make expiation for the sins of the people. For because he himself has suffered and been tempted, he is able to help those who are tempted' (Heb. 2.17, 18). 'For we have not a high priest who is unable to sympathize with our weaknesses, but one who in every respect has been tempted as we are, yet without sinning' (Heb. 4.15).

These are some of the loveliest and most comforting words in the Christian vocabulary: 'Touched with our infirmities', 'tempted as we are'. One of the principles of some of the most effective modern therapies is that the sick make the best healers. This is the principle behind Alcoholics Anonymous and Gamblers Anonymous. It is the principle behind group therapy techniques. The wounded help the wounded. They speak the same language, have had the same experiences. They help to strengthen and heal each other. And this is one of the secrets of the power of Jesus. He *understands* us. He is tempted like as we are. He knows our frailties. 'He knoweth whereof we are made'. He is one of us. Count the ways.

Temptation. Jesus was tempted, put to the test repeatedly. In fact, he probably knew temptation in a way most of us never will. Bishop Westcott pointed out that the person who gives in to temptation immediately, never really knows the power of temptation. He's a pushover. The tempter does not have to exert much pressure on him. All he needs is a little crook of the finger, and he's got him. But the person who resists temptation for a long time will feel the strong impact of the tempter's art, and the person who never gives in will feel the full impact of temptation. The person who holds out to the end knows more about the power of temptation than the pushover who gives in immediately. Jesus, we are told, was 'tempted in every respect as we are, yet without sinning'. The point is that Jesus understands the pressures we are under. He sympathizes.

Sorrow. Jesus has been called 'the man of sorrows'. He knows the sorrows that overwhelm us. He wept at the death of his friend Lazarus: the sorrows of bereavement. He wept over Jerusalem, because it had rejected him: the sorrows of rejection; the sorrows of those who have been discarded by society, by husband or wife or friend; the sorrows of those who are unfulfilled in their lives, emotionally rejected. He knows our sorrows and shares them.

Fear. Jesus was afraid. He was in an agony of fear in the Garden of Gethsemane, and on the cross itself he went through all the anxieties and panic that accompany the loneliness of dying.

So he knows our temptations, sorrows and fears. But he also knows our joys and pleasures. There were people whom he specially loved and loved to be with. There was much that he enjoyed about life, even as he went seriously and urgently about his ministry. He wasn't called 'a gluttonous man, a wine-bibber and a sinner' for nothing.

This, then, is one of the reins we must grip firmly: the humanity of Christ, his solidarity with us in our joys and frailties. There have been times when this rein has been dropped altogether, times when this truth has been eclipsed. Today, we are in no danger of forgetting the humanity of Jesus. Each age has its theological partiality: ours is for the human Jesus, our Jesus, the man for us and for others. When this aspect of the truth about Jesus is stressed, what are some of the consequences?

In theology. The emphasis is very much on this world. Jesus becomes an example of how to live our lives, and he becomes a stimulus towards improving the quality of life. This can lead to what is called 'the social gospel', the application of the example of Jesus to the problems of human society. It can lead to an activist, serving type of discipleship, a discipleship of works. Christians care about the world and about other men and women, because Christ was a man who was tempted, touched with our infirmities.

In the Church. The emphasis, again, is on the human aspect. The Church is a service agency, an advocate on behalf of the needy according to one tradition or, according to another, a kind of social club. Friendship and human interaction are stressed above all else. The humanity of the Church is emphasized.

In Christian behaviour. We find the same emphasis. There is great stress on understanding, and forgiving human sinfulness. Much is made of accepting men and women as they are. Like a good social worker, the Christian tries to avoid being judgemental. He doesn't like too much emphasis on sin.

In the liturgy. The same theme works itself out. Intimacy and informality are stressed. An attempt is made to humanize the liturgy, to make it more accessible to people

This obviously influences the language and the music that is used. And it has an obvious effect on the architecture of churches. Here the emphasis is upon interaction, upon community, upon inter connectedness. The Church may be circular, with the altar in the centre, around which the whole Church revolves. What is lacking in awe and transcendence may be compensated for by the warmth and family feeling that is exuded.

Now, it will be obvious that a proper stress on the humanity of Christ is fundamental, if the Church is to retain warmth and understanding and be accessible to all sorts and conditions of men. It will be equally obvious that to grasp this rein too tightly can lead to an improper distortion. There can be a sloppy, fraternity house or coffee-bar atmosphere about, that never challenges or elevates. There can be a terrible descent into sentimentality, that dishonest emotionalism which can so easily characterize certain types of worship, at one extreme; or into that garrulous, opinionated, aggressive translation of gospel into politics, at the other extreme. Whenever one theological element in the faith is overemphasized at the expense of others, distortions occur.

What, then, is the other rein, the other side to the nature of Christ which the New Testament emphasizes? It is, of course, the divinity of Christ. The central paradox of our faith is that Jesus is both man and God, human and divine, brother and saviour, comforter and judge. According to the Letter to the Hebrews, Jesus is the divine Son who has come to rescue us from our fallen humanity: 'In many and various ways God spoke of old to our fathers by the prophets; but in these last days he has spoken to us by a Son, whom he appointed the heir of all things, through whom also he created the world. He reflects the glory of God and bears the very stamp of his nature, upholding the universe by his word of power' (Heb. 1.1-3). 'Jesus has been counted worthy of as much more glory than Moses as the builder of a house has more honour than the house . . . Now Moses was faithful in all God's house as a servant . . . but Christ was faithful over God's house as a son' (Heb. 3.3-6).

So Jesus is like us; he is also utterly different from us. Something about him draws us towards him in love and friendship; but there is something else about him that makes us fall back in awe and adoration and, yes, in sheer shame: 'Depart from me, for I am a sinful man, O Lord'. You constantly find this note in the Gospel. There is a majesty about Jesus that calls forth something much more than human loyalty, it calls forth worship. This is much more difficult for us to grasp. We know what a man is like. How can we penetrate to the divine, especially when it is conjoined to our humanity? Well, the Church has never been able to explain it, it simply affirms it, proclaims it: 'This we know'. But the Church recognized very early in its history that this was the way it had to be if we were to be changed, not simply understood or comforted. And this brings us to a crucial element in the Christian life, and it is very important to the writer to the Hebrews. Christ came to *change* us. St Athanasius says that Christ became human so that we might become divine. He wants us to grow into the fulness of perfected humanity. He doesn't want us in the spiritual nursery school all our days. Hebrews describes him as the heavenly pioneer who has come to lead us over. So we have to grasp a number of painful contrasts.

Jesus understands our weaknesses more profoundly than we do ourselves, but he wants to bring us through and out of them. He wants to lead us from the valley where we languish, where we acquiesce in our own weakness, up to the mountain tops of sanctification and holiness.

Jesus not only forgives our sins, he offers us the power not to sin. Always, he wants to lead us past the first stages, the elementary principles, through to the solid creation of a new personality, a new character.

In short, Jesus is not only identified with us, he is also identified with God. He came in order to open up for us a way into the divine life. He is not only our brother; he is the divine Son.

This raises a very difficult theological category for many people today, the pre-existence of Christ. According to the classic formulation of our faith, the humanity Jesus assumed did not exist before his birth in Bethlehem; his divine nature had been within the Godhead from all eternity. How can we possibly enter into or understand a truth like that? We can't. Alas, some people go on to conclude that, since they don't understand it, can't get their mind round it, it can't be true. They make their minds the measure of the vast mysteries of truth. They echo words that were said of Benjamin Jowett, famous Master of Balliol:

> 'First come I; my name is Jowett.
> There's no knowledge but I know it.
> I am Master of this College;
> What I don't know isn't knowledge'.

Well, the divinity of Christ is a revealed truth. That is to say, it is a truth that we could not find out for ourselves: it had to be disclosed to us. Next, there is no philosophical reason why it can't be true. The God who created all things, and who influences us from afar, as it were, could, if he chose, assume a different mode of contact with his creation. To deny that is to limit the freedom of the divine nature. A related problem is our linear concept of time. Time is split up into bits for us. But time does not exist in eternity, it is not anything that modifies the divine nature. We have no analogy for that, except for those moments when time has ceased to exist for us, when everything has been reduced to a timeless present. For some reason, time and space are necessary to the purpose of our creation, but God is not limited by them. Rather, they are contained within him. He encloses them. It can't have been more than an elementary problem of divine physics for God to make a specific

101

entrance into time, and to limit and confine some aspects of his nature in order to further his purpose of love.

But people don't reject the incarnation because they don't think God could pull it off. They reject it because the myths and legends and fairy tales of humanity are full of foreshadowings of it. Kings become paupers. Gods die and rise again. Beautiful princesses are found among the cinders and the bootblacking. 'See', they say, 'it is all a fairy tale. This kind of stuff has been around for ages. The Christian claim must be another fairy tale.' This is called 'guilt by association'. Nothing is ever proved, of course. Instead, they sneer it out of existence. Two things can be said about all this.

In the first place, it is breathtakingly illogical to assert that just because things happen in myths and legends they can never happen in fact. It is true that there are lots of fairy tales about nursery school teachers marrying princes, but that does not make the marriage of Charles and Diana any less a fact.

Secondly, is it not just as likely that all those stories are elusive recognitions of a great truth that was in the mind of God before it happened? Myth has to come from somewhere. It comes from that cloudy region where our race is most open to the promptings of the mind of God. The myths could be what C.S. Lewis called 'good dreams', foreshadowings of God's strategy. Myth is one of the ways God sends us ideas. So the fairy tales need not embarrass us, and they might even be true in ways we are now too modern and stupid to understand. Maybe the incarnation is a myth, but it is a true myth. It is a fact that had its origin in the mind of the God who has forever been priming the unconscious mind of our race with dreams and visions, preparing them, getting them ready for that moment which was the intersection of eternity with time.

Now, what happens when the divine nature of Christ is emphasized, when this rein is held tightly?

In theology. There is great emphasis upon the otherness of

102

Christ. He is a glorious and transcendent reality, who calls forth from us the absolute surrender of worship and adoration. He draws us away from the world. It pales beside the splendour of his glory. It is counted as indifferent, as 'refuse' in Paul's phrase. He fills our eyes and our hearts. Who needs anything else?

In the Church. The same emphasis is felt. Worship becomes the great central fact, the reason for the Church's existence. In worship a ladder is set up between heaven and earth, and we ascend it to God.

In Christian behaviour. The emphasis is upon the serious pursuit of perfection. 'Be thou perfect, as thy heavenly father is perfect', the divine Saviour said to us. And history is full of men and women who have followed that advice. They deny themselves. They pray without ceasing. They evangelize with unbelievable and effective intensity. They go through life like spiritual meteors, lighting up their generations.

In liturgy. Again, the emphasis is on the transcendence of Christ. Every effort is made to find a perfect offering in terms of language and music. Jesus is the *Christus Rex*, Christ the King, and our worship becomes a glorious act of homage. Here there is no room for the sloppy and the informal. Here everything is done with the care that is brought into a king's court. And, of course, architecture reflects this, too. The altar is high, distant and lifted up. The whole tendency of the building is to draw one's eyes away from earth to the throne of God.

Again, a proper stress on all this is essential if the Church is to be truly holy, and if it is to have a divine message that will really change and sanctify men and women. Just as obviously, it can be overdone. It can create a stiff, icy rigidity in worship and in character. It can intimidate people, and it can breed a kind of social and spiritual snobbery among Christians.

What is needed is balance. We need to hold each rein with equal firmness and conviction. Sometimes we have to

103

put a touch more emphasis on one side, then on the other, if we are to travel safely and truly. We have to proclaim that sinners are forgiven and that they are called to holiness. We have to know in our weakness that we are understood by Christ our friend and that he would draw us out of our weakness. We have to walk with Jesus as a brother and never forget that one day we shall meet him as our judge.

It is this balance in Christian doctrine that makes it so exciting and so intrinsically wise. We must try not to distort that ancient balance, that creative tension. We must grip both reins and move forward. And as we move forward, we must have Jesus in front of us: 'consider, be attentive to, Jesus, the apostle and high priest of our confession'.

Then Christ starts calling to us, asking us to lift our heads above the current and look towards him. Once we start looking and really seeing, then he begins to draw us towards himself, against the current, against the flood, with other voices in our ears, against other hands that would hold us back, he is drawing us, drawing us towards himself. That, at any rate, is what he longs to do. For it to happen, we have to look at Jesus and see him as he is in himself and not as we have made him or received him or choose to understand him. We have to let him stand before us so that we can really see him; maybe for the first time. We have to learn all over again to look towards Jesus.

8. The Perfect Priest

Bishop Montgomery Campbell, who was well known for his dry and caustic tongue, stood in St Paul's Cathedral in London on a certain diocesan occasion and watched his clergy forming up in procession. Clearly, it was not a pretty sight, and he turned to his chaplain and quoted from the Book of Revelation: 'And the sea shall give up its dead'. Clergy are frequently the target of barbs like that. Down the ages the sacred ministry has provided an endless source of amusement to the impartial observer. We are still to be found affectionately or maliciously lampooned in certain periodicals. *Punch* still trots out cartoons of ineffably silly curates from time to time, though the trendy clergyman probably now rivals the ineffectual curate of the Victorian era as a favourite subject. As Paul remarked, we are a strange spectacle to angels and men. I am always moved and intrigued by the clergy I meet as I stalk them in their native habitat or come upon them in large migratory gatherings. In any large group there are always one or two who are clearly men of great goodness and sanctity. Some are struggling against enormous personal and professional temptations which are part of the very nature of their vocation. Others are mournfully and obsessively aware of their own ineffectiveness, as they struggle with little success to build up their congregation. Others are worldly and full of the dangerous self-confidence that a certain kind of success brings. Some are filled with anger and tormented by tensions within and conflicts without. Quite a few are clearly misfits, using the ministry as a way of working out irresolvable psychological tensions. The clergy are a strange and wistful army, who are never quite sure how they are going to be received as they straggle through history, hated, loved and laughed at, sometimes; perhaps most of the time, just ignored. It's a mysterious calling, and I'd like to think about it.

The Letter to the Hebrews has been called 'the Epistle of Priesthood', because it deals with the priesthood of Jesus. In chapter 5.1 it gives us a very good definition of priesthood: 'Every high priest chosen from among men is appointed to act on behalf of men in relation to God'. In verse four he tells us: 'And one does not take the honour upon himself, but he is called by God'. These texts and others in the epistle define priesthood as a mediating activity. Perhaps the modern example that captures it best is the office of ambassador. An ambassador has a mediating function: he comes from one country to another. He represents his home country to his host country. But he also represents the host country to his own government. He is a mediator, a man on the frontier, on the margin. So is the priest: he acts on behalf of men in relation to God; he leads their prayer and presents their offerings. But God has chosen him to act as his ambassador to men and women. We are ambassadors for Christ, says Paul, pleading with the world, be reconciled to God.

So there are two inseparable aspects of the priestly role. First of all, the priest is a human being, identified with the world. This means he is a sensitive and a sympathetic mediator. As Hebrews says, 'He can deal gently with the ignorant and wayward, since he himself is beset with weakness'. He pleads the weakness of men and women before God. But he is also called to represent God to those same men and women with whom he is identified. Often, an ambassador has to deliver unpleasant news to the people to whom he is sent. The Letter to the Hebrews is full of this tension, this paradox. We have thought about the paradox of the humanity and the divinity of Jesus. Now, we see the same emphasis in a different context, applied to the meaning of priesthood, but it is the same theme: the effectiveness of real priesthood lies in the tension that is created by the priest's loyalty to men and women and his loyalty to God. There is in the priestly life, therefore, an essential humanity, the natural dimension; and there is an essential divinity, the supernatural dimension. If one of these aspects is missing, then real mediation does not take place. In actual priesthood as we have it in history there have been many gradations of type between these poles. I want to look at extreme exaggerations on either side of this mediatorial tension.

First of all, then, you have the priest who is too human, too completely identified with humanity. This over-identification comes in two basic forms: the *amiable* and the *irascible*. Let us look at the amiable priest, the charming and attractive worldling. This priest has some major character flaw. He has a weakness that renders him vulnerable. He may have a drinking problem — many priests do. He may have a sexual problem, some temptation that he succumbs to from time to time. Maybe he's ambitious, and uses his vocation as a career structure. He gets into church politics, starts chasing mitres, the way some members of his congregation chase promotions. Now, priests in any of these categories are often sympathetic and understanding. They know what the world, the flesh and the devil are like. They have a strong fellow-feeling with their parishioners. They are definitely touched with the same infirmities. Sometimes, indeed, they are more infirm than those to whom they are sent. What you get in this situation is the priest as pal or boon companion. He's probably very popular. His parishioners may even be protective towards him. He's gentle and sympathetic, but he never leads them higher than his own level. His own knowledge of his own weaknesses, either consciously or unconsciously, prevents him from placing moral and spiritual challenges before his people. I've known priests who were unadmitted alcoholics, to take but one example, whose drinking problem has held them back from really helping alcoholic parishioners with that tough, loving honesty that is an essential part of the road back to health. There can be something winsome and wistful about the amiably worldly priest. Often he is a tragic figure, divided in his own heart, but excellent company.

Far less attractive is the irascible and worldly priest. He is the opposite of the priest-as-pal. He is impatient to get on with his own projects, so he gets bad tempered at the intrusions people make upon his time. His worldliness may not be as gross as his brother's, but it may be more profound. This type of priest is often intellectual, with strong theological interests and convictions. He is often bored with the petty details that accompany the pastoral ministry. As he gets older, he finds it more and more difficult to suffer fools gladly. Types of the irascible priest abound in Christian history. St Jerome, who translated the Bible into Latin for the first time, is the supreme example. He was in a constant state of irritability. As my own spiritual arteries harden, I fear that this is the type I am turning into, though maybe I don't fear it enough.

Well, if the amiably weak priest is too approachable, too soft and indulgent, the irascibly weak priest becomes increasingly difficult to approach, as he erects barricades round his privacy. The great mystery of grace is that God can still use these flawed and compromised characters. There is a wise and ancient doctrine which holds that the unworthiness of the minister does not invalidate the sacrament. So, that man whose behaviour at last night's party appalled you still mediates the body and blood of Christ to you today; and the man who tore a strip off you last week in an outburst of temper still mediates the forgiveness of Christ.

The worldly priest, the priest who is too human, is the more common type in today's Church, but there is another kind of aberration. This is the priest who is, apparently, so completely identified with God that he has lost touch with humanity. He comes in two forms as well: the *rarefied* and the *severe*. First of all, then, the rarefied. This is the type of priest who is hypersensitive and super-spiritual. People are reluctant to approach him because they feel he can't possibly understand their very basic difficulties. As they are likely to say of him: 'He is so heavenly minded that he's no earthly use'. Very often, this hyperspirituality and sensitivity is a natural endowment rather than the supernatural result of intense spiritual struggle. Something that Geoffrey Faber said of the famous Victorian clergyman, Dean Stanley, sums up what I'm trying to get at very well: 'Stanley was not a mystic. He did not set out to discipline or to mortify his senses: they merely withered away. The "purity of heart and life which those who knew him best considered to be the distinguishing quality of his character and career" was not a deliberate conquest of the old Adam. It was a defect, a negative, cutting him off from any comprehension of the animal affirmatives in which human nature is founded'.[1] The rarefied priest is perceived by people as being of little use to them, because he lives in a different world. People don't approach him, because they think it would be a waste of time.

And they don't approach the severely spiritual priest, because he scares them or makes them feel guilty. This type of priest has mortified and suppressed his senses, often in a struggle so severe that a certain harshness of character results. Some of the greatest saints have been of this type. Their own struggles give them a bit of a down on humanity and its weaknesses. They lose the gentleness of which Hebrews speaks. They can be harsh and spiritually demanding in their dealings with others. They have something of the hardness and loneliness of the prophet about them. They do not make popular parish priests.

Now, I have painted the extremes. There are many gradations in between. The point I am trying to make is a simple one, however: no human priest ever achieves the perfect balance between heaven and earth, God and humanity. We all fluctuate wildly, erring in one direction or the other. Balance is the hardest thing to achieve in life, and the real priest is the perfectly balanced character: gentle, but severe when necessary; filled with tenderness, yet capable of righteous anger against all that opposes God and his holiness. One of the great themes of Hebrews is that only Jesus fulfils this description: he is the only perfect priest, the only real mediator. He is the perfect mediator because he is perfectly God and perfectly man, able to achieve perfect mediation, perfect balance between the divine and the human.

The drama and anguish of the human priest's life is the struggle to conform himself to the priesthood of Christ, so that his likeness may be formed in him, so that he becomes 'another Christ' or, rather, so that Christ may perform his eternal and priestly ministry through him. Bishop Ken wrote some lines that describe 'The Good Priest':

Give me the priest these graces shall possess —
Of an Ambassador the just address;
A father's tenderness, a shepherd's care;
A leader's courage who the cross can bear;
A ruler's arm, a watchman's wakeful eye;
A pilot's skill, the helm in storms to ply;
A fisher's patience, and a labourer's toil;
A guide's dexterity to disembroil;
A prophet's inspiration from above;
A teacher's knowledge and a Saviour's love.

Very few in any generation achieve the perfect balance and equilibrium of the priestly character, but they look to Christ that he may, however slowly, finish the work he has begun in them.

I am sure that an essential part of the renewal of the Church in our generation must be the recovery of the integrity of priesthood. For a variety of reasons, some of which have to do with the perfectly valid recovery of a proper theology of lay ministry, and some of which have to do with the role crisis that has afflicted the ordained ministry in the last twenty years, there has been a failure of nerve in the ordained priesthood, and many of us have been uttering strange and uncertain sounds to our increasingly bewildered people. I would like to suggest two matters that ought to be at the top of our agenda for action as we move with renewed confidence into the years ahead: the recovery of preaching and the recovery of priestly spirituality, as contemporary modes or extensions of the incarnation.

Bernard Manning described preaching as 'a manifestation of the incarnate Word, from the written word, by the spoken word'. Preaching, then, is an extension of the incarnation, it is one of the ways God has chosen to continue his presence among his children. It is a manifestation of the incarnate Word, made word again, through the stumbling affirmations of those he has called to preach. In preaching, when it is faithfully and passionately done, a mysterious interchange takes place. There is a communication between God and the listener, and this communication is not just from the preacher. It is not his words that convict and save: it is the Word of God himself who addresses those who hear, through the mediation of the preacher. And this is no proud claim made by preachers. It is a terrifying fact. It is a burden that makes preachers not as other men are, for they bear about with them the contagion of God. They are touched, in spite of themselves, with the divine anguish, the longing of God to reach his children. It is a terrifying vocation. A smug preacher is a contradiction in terms, because he carries in his soul the secret of God's sorrow and love. Preachers are set apart to manifest the incarnate Word.

Manning goes on, 'it is a manifestation of the incarnate Word from the written word'. We are to be men of the Bible, interpreters of those flaming and baffling words. We are to live with those written words, day in and day out. We are not to preach ourselves, Christ is to be preached through us, from those traditions that are handed on to us.

111

We are to interrogate the text in such a way that the answer of God can be heard, and not simply the echo of our own preconceptions. We are to ask questions of the New Testament, indeed, but we must take heed how we ask. It is possible to ask, like Pilate, and not wait for an answer. It is possible to ask and ask, like a sadistic policeman, until you get the answer you want. And it is possible to ask in the way one pumps a friend for news from relatives she's just visited, eager for every detail, seeking somehow to make those you love present again. In our preaching we are to manifest the incarnate Word from the written word, by a lifetime of contemplation and study, by a lifetime of patient waiting for the Word to manifest himself through the words of the tradition.

Finally, preaching 'is a manifestation of the incarnate Word, from the written word, by the *spoken* word.' By *our* words! We are to wield them well. We are to take risks. We are not to be afraid of the divine foolishness. Above all, we are not to be afraid of emotion in the pulpit. After all, what could be more affecting than the story of the everlasting sorrow of God, searching for his lost children down all time's days? There's one last paradox I'd like to mention. The preacher achieves his closest identification with Christ when his own heart breaks, when he discovers the essentially tragic nature of his vocation. Like the clown, he has to deliver his lines, whether or not he feels like it. He is not immune to personal temptation and radical doubt, yet he is called to preach in season and out of season. Preachers often find themselves assailed by radical doubt, just after they have defended or justified some great doctrine. They find themselves more tempted, just after they have delivered some great call to holiness. Yet they must go on. They preach not themselves. They are called, by their words, to make the incarnate Word manifest. Often, like the clown with the broken heart, they have to deceive in order to be true, they have to allow themselves to be used by God, even on days when their own minds, their own

112

lives are in rebellion against him. So preachers are figures of contradiction, God's fools, clowns, and in the Church there have to be clowns.

As important as the recovery of preaching, and closely related to it, is the recovery of prayer in the priestly life. Perfunctory preachers are usually perfunctory prayers. Yet it is in the life of prayer that staleness and fatigue so often afflict the priest. Mountain climbers in deep snow are sometimes overwhelmed by a peculiar lassitude and inertia. They long to lie down and cease to struggle, but to do so is death. A similar affliction possesses the person who struggles in the spiritual life. The desert fathers called it *akedia*, 'the sickness that destroyeth in the noon day.' That peculiar and chronic form of inertia, that centrifugal force that pulls us into our own selves and stops us moving, works with peculiar power right here at the most important part of the ordained minister's life. George McLeod once referred to the bankruptcy corner in every minister's library where lie all those books on prayer that he hoped might help. It is worth casting your mind over your own bankruptcy corner: some tattered Catholic manuals; Bede Frost on Mental Prayer, perhaps; almost certainly, something on the Jesus Prayer; a book or two by Anthony Boom; Mother Julian, maybe; if we're very serious, or know a good second-hand bookshop, there will be the collected works of St John of the Cross and St Teresa of Avila; you'll find a lot of Evelyn Underhill in some corners; maybe a book or two on Christian yoga or Zen for the Christian. We'll have a go at anything that'll give us a bit of a lift. And there they lie, mute witnesses to dreams and longings that are largely unrealized. Yet we must take those dreams out again, we must rekindle those longings, because our ministry, our priesthood is derivative and reflective of the ministry, the priesthood of Christ. It is his ministry, not ours. It is his ministry that works through the priest, and that ministry pulls in and it sends out. The magnetism of the beauty and glory of Christ draws men

113

and women to him. Christ is not without witnesses. In their struggles priests often feel that if they don't persuade people, then people will forget all about Christ, and the rumour of God will die out. But it won't. God is still active, can still work directly. He is not bound to us! In the Old Testament there is no explicit call to mission. The emphasis is predominantly that of magnetism rather than mission, drawing in, rather than sending out. The great text is Isaiah.

> It shall come to pass in the latter days that the mountain of the house of the Lord shall be established as the highest of the mountains, and shall be raised above the hills; and all the nations shall flow to it, and many peoples shall come, and say: 'Come, let us go up to the mountain of the Lord, to the house of the God of Jacob; that he may teach us his ways and that we may walk in his paths'. For out of Zion shall go forth the law, and the word of the Lord from Jerusalem.
>
> (Isa. 2.2)

The idea was that the people of God would be so attractive, like a city set on a hill, that the nations would be drawn to Zion by its sheer beauty. In the New Testament, in addition to this evangelism by magnetism, of attraction, there is an evangelism of searching, of going out, but the magnetic model is not thereby superseded. It is still an essential element of the Church's impact on the world: 'I, when I am lifted up, will draw all men unto me'. When priests become channels for Christ, conduits for his power, icons of his beauty, they will draw young men and maidens, old men and children to Christ, for all mankind has a thirst, a longing after the holiness of the beauty of God. In the life of prayer the priest decreases so that the character of Jesus may increase in him. There is a yoga phrase about only the empty cup being filled: as we lie, emptied of all false self-confidence, he fills us with himself, so that he can work through us in his address to his children. The priestly life of prayer is not a private consolation; it is an essential part of the missionary strategy of God, so that the image of Christ might be formed in us.

Most priests will agree, rather guiltily, with what I have said, but they are likely to point out that God has thrown them into an insanely hectic life that permits of little prayer and less study. How, then, can they find the time required for the waiting that is an essential prelude to truly incarnational preaching? Where is the space to be found for the great waiting on God in prayer? Most of us have a compulsive need to be available always to everyone; to be engaged in some kind of activity. Ours is a ministry of perspiration, not inspiration. Being still and doing nothing makes us feel guilty. But all the time we allow this pattern to persist we are damaging the showing-forth of Christ in us, we are obscuring him behind the dust and buzz of our lives. I think it was St Bernard who said, 'My exercise of piety must be inviolable. It is even in the interest of those against whom I close my door that I guard it so jealously. And the time thus preserved must be inviolable, quiet.' It is there, unknown to us, that the image of Christ is formed and makes its appeal through us. How can we free priests from the tyranny of their own busyness and persuade them that they really ought to go into their chambers and close the door and pray to their Father who is in secret? How can we get them to do that, how can we get ourselves to do it? How can we help the Church to be quiet? 'Poor little talkative Christianity', said E.M. Forster. Like all compulsive talkers, are we anxious about what might happen when we stopped filling in the gaps made by the strange silences of God? Are we anxious in case, if we won't speak up for him, no one else will? Fr Kelly said: 'He who cannot keep silence is not content with God, for God's voice speaks most often in silence'. How can we help that silence grown in ourselves, in the Church, so that God's voice can be heard?

115

I have really been trying to make one point: as priests, we do not proclaim ourselves or draw people to or by ourselves — that might, indeed does, happen, but what we then produce is a human cult, not the family of Christ. No, we preach not ourselves, but through us Christ reaches out to those who are his own, and that happens only as we abide in him and his life flows through us. That abiding happens in the Eucharist and the divine office and private prayer, and in our wrestling with the meaning and the reality of Christ, our great high priest.

And none of this applies exclusively to ordained priests. There is a priesthood in which all believers share, the priesthood of the Church. The Church is called to be the world's priest, to represent God to humanity and humanity to God. Every Christian is an ambassador of that same cause, called to mediate, in his own person, between the demands of earth and the claims of heaven, called, in some sense, to be a bridge between heaven and the high street.

9. The Folly of Preaching

I want to say more about preaching since it continues to be the main method of Christian apologetics. Preaching, like marriage, is an endless source of innocent amusement; but like marriage again, it is easier to point out its many weaknesses than to come up with a really adequate alternative. I want, however, to make a limitation upon the topic and be descriptive rather than prescriptive. In other words, I want to examine how preaching is done, rather than suggest ways in which it ought to be done. To do this I want to divide this chapter into three parts, following Hegel's celebrated dialectical process of thesis, antithesis and synthesis, though my main emphasis will be upon the first two for a very good reason. In the Hegelian method thesis is succeeded by an opposing or contradictory antithesis, and through the ensuing conflict the two are brought together again at a higher level as synthesis. In preaching, this final synthesis is eschatological: it is not achieved by us. In other words, in the Church there are preachers of thesis, thetic preachers, and there are preachers of antithesis, antithetic preachers: there is but one who brings these together in a transcending synthesis.

Moreover, each type or level of preaching is associated with certain doctrinal paradigms: each is rooted, either explicitly or implicitly, in certain of the Christian doctrines. Preachers, without being consciously aware of it, are selective in their use of Christian doctrine. Christian doctrine is a vast and paradoxical and dazzling enterprise, full of thunder and lightning and dark mountain peaks from which torrents and cataracts pour down in frightening force; and full, also, of quiet valleys filled with sunlight and butterflies and laughter and peace. Christian doctrine terrifies and consoles; it damns and redeems. Christian preaching does the same: some preachers are comforters, sons of consolation; others are theological terrorists, disturbers of the peace. Thesis and antithesis. I want to begin with thesis.

The spoken or unspoken assumption behind thetic preaching is this: there is closeness and continuity between God and his creation; God is immanent in his creation. The doctrinal paradigms are obvious and so are the texts upon which they are based. The doctrine of creation is the foundation, and the text is from Genesis: 'In the beginning God created the heavens and the earth . . . and God saw everything that he had made, and behold, it was very good' (Genesis 1.1,31). And the doctrine of the incarnation builds upon this foundation, for the very Word that brought forth creation comes to its own: 'And the Word was made flesh and dwelt among us' (John 1.14). Now, if you take these doctrines seriously they have a profound effect upon your attitude to the world and to history. Many Christians, especially if they are priests, professional exponents of the faith, have a conspiracy theory of the world: it is hostile to them and their convictions, it has no comprehension of what they are saying. Well, if you believe in the creation and incarnation and the immanence of God in history the picture is dramatically altered: God is already out there ahead of you; he is, in Augustine's word, prevenient. He has gone ahead to prepare the ground, so that when we approach the world and the men and women who live in it, they are already predisposed to hear the word of God. This predisposition may even become blazingly explicit, without the aid of the professional consultant, the God-botherer, as an agnostic friend of mine calls priests. A remarkable survey conducted in the USA underlines this. Andrew M.

Greely, the programme director of the Centre for the Study of American Pluralism at the National Opinion Research Centre, University of Chicago, and William C. McGready, the associate programme director, discovered, almost by accident, that a number of people they knew had had mystical experiences. They managed to find room in 'a representative national survey of ultimate values among some 1,500 American adults for a handful of questions on mystical experiences'. They were staggered by the response. 'About 600 persons — two-fifths of the 1,500 asked the question — reported having at least one such experience.' Similar results have been obtained in British surveys.

Now, I don't want to depend too heavily upon this data, but it does underline one of the points I am seeking to establish: the Christian apologist is not operating in foreign territory; nor, apparently, does God depend entirely upon human intermediaries in making himself known to men and women. He is quite capable of making a direct approach to individuals. It does seem to be true that 'in him we live and move and have our being'. And this has a profound effect upon the preacher who believes it. Like Paul on Mars Hill, his task will be to declare the true identity of one whom people already know; he will seek to draw their attention to the logic of their own experience. So the preacher is an interpreter, or a man who makes connections that other people might be missing. Another word for this is poetry. The preacher is a poet who celebrates the divine glory that blazes through creation. He does not essentially tell people what they do not already know, so much as show them the meaning and the depth of their own experience. He calls them to stop, look and listen, to see and hear what God is doing in their midst.

The thesis that lies behind this type of preaching has an important effect not only upon the content of preaching, but upon its form. Indeed, it would not be going too far to say that for this type of preaching the method is just as

119

important as the message because, by definition, God has chosen to make himself present in the very forms that disclose his meaning. In abstract terms there may be a difference and a distance between God and his creation, but from our point of view he comes to us through it, and how are we to separate the disclosure-situation from the one who is disclosed? We cannot. He comes to us in, through and by means of our experience: and we can't experience God apart from our experience. Our experience of him is our experience. So this type of preacher will lay enormous stress upon existence as parable or symbol. Here, of course, the great exemplar for the preacher is our Lord himself, who taught in parables. Teaching in parables has two related aspects. First of all, it is a communication method, a teaching device. It is a way of capturing attention. A parable arrests the attention because it begins where people are and leads them on. The parable hooks them, and they are taken on from it to a connection they had never made before. So this type of preaching lays enormous stress upon the opening of the sermon. It is at this point that the most important thing happens: the arrestment of attention. If attention is not captured, the rest is in vain. And here the committed preacher is prepared to go to any lengths, even of vulgarity or bad taste, to capture the attention of his hearers. The opening arrest, of course, will be closely related to the situation of the hearers. Studdert Kennedy captured the attention of the soldiers he preached to in the Great War by leaning over the edge of the pulpit and swearing at them. Dick Shepherd did something similar when he hung a red lamp outside St Martin in the Fields, just like the ones that hung outside the brothels behind the lines in France in the Great War. Both spoke in parables. Both began where their hearers were and then led them to the moment of disclosure and meaning. Preaching of this sort is often eighty per cent introductory formula or arrestment technique, and twenty per cent hard substance. The masters of this art show a lack of fastidiousness and self-consciousness that is rare in the Anglican preacher. They will go to any lengths to gain a hearing, a form of heroism rare in Anglican circles, where good taste frequently muzzles the good news. Our Church is not famous for its redemptive vulgarity. But this form of preaching by story and illustration, by attention-getting devices of many sorts, is not just a communication method, a device to capture people's attention so that you can then sock the real message to them. It is itself a revelatory message, because it depends upon the assumption that God is coming to us all the time in everything that is: he speaks to us, always, in parables. These are the ways he is disclosing himself to us. The parable announces the fact that God is there, if only we'll connect. This kind of preacher really does see a world alive with the grandeur of God. Anything he touches speaks of God because God is latent within it. The Canon of Scripture becomes as wide as the universe and revelation is a permanent adventure.

It follows from all this that this type of preacher will be a man of the world. He will be very much at home in culture and society; nothing will be alien to him. He'll be an avid student of newspapers and the latest good novel. He'll know what is happening in the film industry and the world of the theatre. Above all, he'll be a reader, perhaps a writer, of poetry. In all these ways he'll participate in and identify with the culture and society of his time, and he'll feel in all this the promptings of God and see in the movements of history the pressure of the Holy Spirit. He'll tend to be enthusiastic about experiments in human relations, because he'll see the hand of God here, too. He'll take very seriously our Lord's promise to be with two or three who are gathered in his name, and he'll accord almost revelational value to group work and the latest therapy and self-discovery technique.

And behind it all is the assumption that God is close to his creation and still at work within it. Let me now try to give you a thumbnail sketch of this type of preacher. In

William James' terminology, he will tend to the 'once-born' type of psychological make-up: warm and amiable and unanxious in his dealings with others. In the pulpit he'll be affirmative and supportive; he'll rarely scold. He's not likely to adopt extreme moral attitudes that are likely to make him unpopular with his parishioners. He'll enjoy the world without necessarily being worldly, though often he is. In fact, and like many an Anglican before him, he is a good-natured, relaxed and friendly pelagian and his deficiencies are as obvious as his merits. He is very deficient in the tragic sense of life, which is why he'll have more appeal for the achievers of this world than for the losers (this is one reason among others why he'll often be found in the wealthier suburbs). He often makes a good priest, but rarely a prophet. There is little real challenge in what he has to say; no sense of judgement; nothing stark or terrifying. He won't be much good in situations of social confusion or historical crisis, mainly because he has become so identified with the culture that he can no longer achieve a critical detachment from it. If it came to it, he'd probably end up burning incense to Caesar, though he'd carefully work out a clever and perfectly sincere justification for doing so beforehand. Let us leave him for the moment without judging him (who of us, anyway, has the right to judge?) and move on to his opposite number.

The spoken or unspoken assumption behind antithetic preaching is this: there is a vast qualitative distance between God and his creation; God immensely transcends and is discontinuous with his creation. Again, the doctrinal paradigms are obvious and so are the texts upon which they are based. The doctrine of the fall is foundational and there is, again, a text from Genesis: '. . . the Lord God sent him forth from the garden of Eden, to till the ground from which he was taken. He drove out the man.' (Genesis 3.23-24). And if the fall antithetically balances the creation, so does the passion of Christ balance the incarnation: 'He came to his own and his own received him not' (John 1.11).

Therefore, says Paul, '. . . the wrath of God is revealed from heaven against all ungodliness and wickedness of men who by their wickedness suppress the truth' (Romans 1.18). Now if you take these doctrines seriously; if you experience them as true because you have gazed upon the sinfulness and selfishness and cruelty of humankind, your attitudes to history and human possibility will be profoundly modified. You'll believe that man has a rooted and pathological aversion to the truth and is fatally attracted to error. Not only is his moral nature radically flawed; his intellectual, rational faculties are hopelessly biased, too. This chronic complex of disorder not only turns man against his neighbours, it places a vast gulf between himself and God. There can be no knowledge of God that is achieved by a good-natured process of evolution. There is no such thing as spiritual gradualism. Man is brought to the knowledge of God, when he is brought at all, by a conclusive act of the divine mercy that is convulsive in its consequence for man: it either redeems him or declares him damned. But even when he is saved, man still stands under sentence of nothingness: he is always in a state of futility and weakness, prone always to that idolatry which is the main characteristic of human culture. Paul goes on: '. . . they are without excuse; for although they knew God they did not honour him as God or give thanks to him, but they became futile in their thinking and their senseless minds were darkened. Claiming to be wise, they became fools, and exchanged the glory of the immortal God for images . . .' (Romans 1.20-23). And don't make the mistake of thinking the Letter to the Romans is only about the past. It is horrifyingly contemporary. It always has been, which is one reason why it tends to be behind all the great turning points in Christian history.

So the antithetic preacher is a man against the times, not a man who is submerged in them. He is the man against the culture, not the man of culture. He stands permanently upon watch and observes with melancholy relish the ease with which superficial and naive Christians are taken in by the society in which they are set, and exchange the glory of God for images, idols. His reading of history confirms him in this depressing judgement: the Church is invariably taken over by the spirit of the age and becomes a mere adjunct of the culture or a chaplain to the powerful, whether men or ideas. He sees the phenomenon of medieval Christendom as the triumph of the Roman Empire over Jesus Christ. He contemplates the many occasions on which national churches have consecrated the values of their host societies: the Church of England as the Conservative Party at prayer in eighteenth- and nineteenth-century England; the craven weakness of the Evangelical Church in Nazi Germany; the way in which American Christianity is slavishly sensitive to the pervading culture and frequently rewrites its whole theological basis to bring it into line with the prevailing ethos; the way in which the Dutch Reformed Church provides spiritual sanction for the racist values of Afrikaanerdom. And many, many others. He sees time and history and human culture as permanently at enmity with God, and he stands upon his watch to warn and denounce, to prophesy in the name of the Lord.

In the pulpit the antithetic preacher will make no concessions to the humanity of his hearers, for it is that very humanity which is their greatest danger. He will not seek to explain the gospel, so much as to proclaim it. Indeed, it is more radical, even, than that, for he believes that the Word of God has autonomous power to convict mankind. He expounds only the Word of God as found in Scripture, allowing it to challenge man by its very contrariness and obscurity. No human word can save. Only the Word of God. And he seeks to bring his hearers to that knowledge of their own nakedness and imprisonment and poverty which is the human prelude to the divine act. Our Lord is the model for this fierce prophetism: not the tender Christ, but the Christ of the withering denunciation; not the Christ who receives sinners, but the Christ who tells them to depart from him into the fire prepared; not the lyrical Christ of the sparrows and the lilies of the field, but the harsh Christ whose tongue cut like a sword; not the Christ who explained everything in parables, but the Christ who preached with baffling opacity, lest his hearers might turn and be saved.

Yes, the antithetic preacher is uncomfortable and infuriating. He goes round like an enraged terrorist, throwing kerygmatic parcel bombs through the doors of the comfortable and efficient temples of Laodicea. In a mysterious way the antithetic preacher needs opposition and hostility the way the thetic preacher needs popularity and acceptance. And he gets it! He sets people's teeth on edge and they often rise up against him and cast him out of the temple. Needless to say, the antithetic preacher rarely makes it in the suburbs, or only in those where there is a heavy concentration of masochists: then you get the contemporary equivalent of the medieval flagellant movement. But that's rare. Few people enjoy being whipped, even by a holy man, so the prophetic preacher tends to be an itinerant. He moves round a lot. He may not even hold down a permanent job, or he may be an associate professor in a seminary. He is more likely to be a curate than a rector, and if he is a bishop then he's almost certainly a bishop-in-exile. Angular and uneasy, he goes through the land carrying on the Lord's controversy with his people, haunted by abandoned Eden.

Let me now try to give you a thumbnail sketch of this type of preacher. In William James' terminology, he will tend to the 'twice-born' type of psychological make-up: harsh and often judgemental, he tends to make people feel guilty because he holds out to them and often in himself exemplifies an impossibly high standard. He is usually lonely, though he may have around him a small group of fanatical adherents. About him there is a whiff of the wilderness, an air from the desert, and a sense of disturbance that sends shivers through those who are at ease in Sion. He may be unpopular in his time, but he is the man for a time of crisis and history frequently vindicates him. His detachment from the culture and his frequent contempt for it save him from that infidelity that frequently overcomes the Church in history. History is usually kinder to him than his contemporaries. But he, being human, suffers from many deficiencies, chief of which is a lack of humour, especially about himself. He is often self-righteous and unfeeling in his personal relations. Reinhold Niebuhr, who was himself touched by the prophetic fire, summed it up better than anyone else I know: 'Whenever a prophet is born, either inside or outside of the church, he faces the problem of preaching repentance without bitterness and of criticizing without spiritual pride . . . Think of sitting Sunday after Sunday under some professional holy man who is constantly asserting his egotism by criticizing yours. I would rebel if I were a layman. A spiritual leader who has too many illusions is useless. One who has lost his illusions about mankind and retains his illusions about himself is insufferable. Let the process of disillusionment continue until the self is included. At that point, of course, only religion can save from the enervation of despair. But it is at that point that true religion is born.' [1] Let us leave him for the moment, without judging him (who of us, anyway, has the right to judge?), and move on.

These two types of preachers do not provide us with a solution to the human problem: they are, in essence, a statement of that problem. I believe that they are reflections, embodiments of the divine ambivalence towards man. God both loves us and rages against us; he wills that all shall be saved, yet he is offended by our righteousness, our truly terrifying lack of care for each other. In thesis and antithesis God's love wrestles with his justice, and the same drama is played out in our hearts. And every preacher longs to achieve that reconciliation, that transcending synthesis that brings the two parts together, but he cannot: he comforts when he should terrify, and he terrifies when he

126

should comfort. Somehow, he never seems able to offer the whole gospel to the whole man. This is the anguish of the preacher, the source of the deep sorrow that is found at the bottom of the heart of the true preacher. The preacher longs to save his hearers, but he can't. He can't even save himself. It is Jesus Christ who is the saviour, even of preachers. In him the priest and the prophet come together. In him love and justice meet and become one. But not by some abstract process of formal logic: he does not resolve the paradox with a form of words — instead, he dies: he takes the struggle, the ambivalence, into the silence of that terrible death and God brings the synthesis out of it. He builds a new creation. We call it the resurrection body, and we do not at all understand it; but we know that in him the two become one. He is the at-one-ment, the synthesis. He is the sermon we all long to preach but never can. He is the Word we can never utter. But the releasing thing is that we don't have to! He is God's Word and he makes his way through creation, picking his way round and through and sometimes even into the simplicities and stridencies of the peculiar company of preachers. I daresay we'll go on scolding and consoling, weeping and rejoicing. Thank God that while we, as usual, are making fools of ourselves, he is saving the world.

EPILOGUE

Paradise Row

Some months ago I went to visit a Cistercian abbey in western Massachusetts. It was a very evocative and nostalgic visit for me. When I was a romantic young Anglo-Catholic Christian I had wanted to be a Cistercian monk. Part of the desire was undoubtedly simple romance and love of the Middle Ages. I loved the very idea of severe monastic churches filled with the sound of plainsong from choirs of cowled monks. I loved the very architecture of monasteries. Visiting some bare ruined choir, the present dissolved for me, and I saw the walls rebuilt and monks going about their eternal task. I was caught by the romance of the cloister. But there was more to it than that. When I was young I had scribbled a quotation from Ernest Renan into my commonplace book:

> The essential element of the Celt's poetic life is adventure; that is to say, the pursuit of the unknown; an endless quest after an object every flying from desire. It was of this that St Brendan dreamed, that Peradur sought with mystic chivalry . . . The race desires the infinite, it thirsts for it, and pursues it at all costs, beyond the tomb, beyond hell itself.

This is one of the great themes and objects of Catholic Christianity: this quest for the absolute, this longing for absolute self-surrender. It can capture a young man's imagination, so that he thinks it is an easy matter. He thinks in terms of the grand gesture of renunciation, not at all of the years of unremitting martyrdom that it requires.

He wants his manhood taken into God in a single, gloriously orchestrated moment, preferably before an adoring and approving audience that shivers at his transcendent heroism.

Well, I spent a large part of my youth and early manhood with a religious community, but, for reasons I think I'd better not go into, I was asked to leave, so I never became a monk. Next, there were dreams and visions of my life thrown away in the service of God in Africa as a missionary. I spent two years there and had opportunity to return, but I never went back. Next came the slums. Fired by the exploits of the great Anglo-Catholic slum priests of the nineteenth century, I longed to give my life to the service of the poor. I spent years in the slums of Glasgow and Edinburgh, but that never became my life work either. And here I am now, in the middle of life's way, comfortably situated, plenty to eat, well clothed, living in a house the size of a small hotel in the most expensive part of Boston, with an interesting job and a happy family. Those dreams of absolute abandonment of myself to God seem very far away. It takes more than a romantic impulse to achieve the reality of heroic sanctity. Every boy wants to be a hero, but most of us grow up to be ordinary and unheroic — though now and again we are visited by the old longings and wonder how it might have been.

Now, I offer that bit of autobiography, not to satisfy an unhealthy appetite for public self-abasement, but as a parable. There is in all of us an absolute longing to give ourselves utterly away in some great cause or for some great love. If the cause be great enough men and women will give themselves to it: they'll leave home and comfort for the sake of the cause. They'll lay down their lives for it. The appetite is there and when the thing that fed it is taken from them people look back wistfully at the days of their glory and self-denial. There is in all of us an urge to sacrifice, to follow an absolute cause, to give our lives away to something great. It is an eternal need that lies sleeping within us till the bugles call it out to gird itself for battle. There's something in us 'wants war, wants wounds', in Hopkins' phrase.

But there's something else in us as well. There's something that wants to stay at home, amidst the comfort of the known and the familiar. Bugles thrill us but they frighten us, too, send shivers of apprehension through us, because they would draw us away from much we hold dear. We long to go on the quest, but we dread that last, long look at home and its blue remembered hills. We want to be adventurers, but our heart winces at what we must give up. We want God but we are afraid, in Francis Thompson's words, 'Lest, having Him, we must have nought beside'. Have you never felt the wintry summons of God and rushed away from it into some warm and noisy and careless place, because already it made you feel a terrible loneliness?

Surely, this is the great theme of Christianity and it corresponds to the double nature of Christ: the divine and the human; the supernatural and the natural. These are kept in a permanent tension in the Christian life. Our life as Christians is an attempt to supernaturalize the natural, and to naturalize the supernatural, to bring our nature up to God, and to bring God into our natural life. So there are two poles in our spiritual life, what Baron von Hügel called the homely and the heroic, the natural and the supernatural. Church history is the story of that tension, because there are always those who stress the supernatural, who want to heighten the Christian standard, make it severe and exclusive and demanding; and there are others who want to make it more easy for common clay like ours to find room in the Church, so they tend to soften and diminish the Christian demand. You know the kind of thing: 'How to follow Christ without leaving home. Christianity without tears'. And Anglicans are very good at this kind of thing. We rarely offend in the heroic direction by making our religion too severe. We err in the homely direction, by creating a version of Christianity that is domestic, familiar, intensely local. That is why John Henry Newman left us in

1845. Dean Church, in his obituary of Newman in the Times, said that he had ever sought to return to the heroic ardour and self-surrender of primitive Christianity. He writes:

> . . . What was there like the New Testament or even the first ages now? Alas, there was nothing completely like them, but of all unlike things the Church of England with its 'smug parsons' and pony carriages for their wives and daughters, seemed to him the most unlike; more unlike than the great unreformed Roman Church with its strange, unscriptural doctrines and its undeniable crimes and alliances, whenever it could, with the world. But at least the Roman Church had not only preserved but maintained at full strength through the centuries to our day two things of which the New Testament was full and which are characteristic of it — devotion and self-sacrifice. The crowds at a pilgrimage, a shrine or a 'pardon' were much more like the multitudes who followed our Lord about the hills of Galilee — like them probably in their imperfect faith which we call superstition — than anything that could be seen in the English Church even if the Salvation Army were one of its instruments.

So again and again we need to set before ourselves the other side of our Faith that we are so prone to neglect. As ordinary, not very heroic Christians, we ought to meditate on the heroic dimension of our faith and try to let it influence us, even though we know quite well that it will never dominate us, never tear us out of ourselves into a life of absolute self-surrender. And surely this is the only really useful purpose behind our observance of the sesquicentennial of the Oxford Movement. The Oxford Movement operated on a number of levels, but at its heart it was a reaffirmation of the heroic side of the Christianity, it was a call to supernatural sanctity, to self-surrender, to costly yet joyous Christianity. And, you know, the really heroic phase of the movement was never in Oxford at all. That is where the flame was kindled, certainly, but the real adventure lay in the carrying of that flame to the ends of the earth. Listen to the words of Henry Scott Holland.

There are few moments more dramatic in our Religious History than the recovery in the Slums by the Oxford Movement of what it had lost in the University. How final that loss looked in Oxford itself can only be realized by those who have heard people like Edward King, of Lincoln, or Oakley, Dean of Manchester, tell of the dark days, when nothing remained of the Movement but the faint flickering flame on the altar at St Mary's which the loyalty of Charles Marriot still sustained in life. Pusey had been silenced. Newman had gone: and, in his going, had swept the place clean. The Heads of Colleges and the Dean were busy stamping out the last embers, by refusing Tutorships to known Tractarians, and by bullying the few Catholic Undergraduates who clung to Charles Marriot at St Mary's. They saw their triumph come. The Provost of Oriel, the President of St John's, the four Tutors, went about at large seeking whom they should devour. The Cause was lost. So it seemed. When lo! it suddenly took on an entirely fresh lease of life. It made a new departure. It was to be heard of in all sorts of unexpected places. It wore unanticipated shapes, and spoke a different language. It had ceased to be Academic. It had become popular. It offered itself to every kind of novel opportunity and risk. It plunged into the dark places of our awful cities. It spent itself, with sacrificial ardour, in the service of the Poor. It shirked nothing: it feared nothing. It took blows and insults with a smile. It went ahead, in spite of menace and persecution. It spoke home to sinning souls and broken hearts, fast bound in misery and iron. It invaded the strongholds of Sin. It itself wore poverty as a cloak, and lived the life of the suffering and the destitute. It was irresistible in its élan, in its pluck, in its thoroughness, in its buoyancy, in its self-abandonment, in its laughter, in its devotion. Nothing could hold it. It won, in spite of all that could be done by Authorities in High Places, or by rabid Protestant Mobs, to drive it under.[1]

There were three great manifestations of that new spirit of heroic self-offering which Canon Scott Holland celebrated in this passage. There was the rediscovery of the religious life. There was the reaffirmation of the missionary vocation. And there was the taking of the faith, in Holland's words, 'into the dark places of our awful cities'. The story of this part of the Catholic Renewal Movement in world Anglicanism is essentially a saga, an adventure, a tale of heroism. It was never at its real best just a fuss about ceremonial and what were called in the Anglo-Catholic underworld, 'full privileges'. I thing we probably ought to admit that many of the ritualistic squabbles were plain childish, on both sides of the dispute. I have a great deal of sympathy with Bishop Mandell Creighton who, as Bishop of London at the height of the Ritualistic Controversy, was helped into an early grave by the intransigence of extremists on both sides. During an interview with a group of Anglo-Catholic clergy he urged his hearers to give up what seemed to him a matter of personal preference for the sake of peace, when one of them said, 'But, my Lord, you must remember that we have a cure of souls.' To which came the quick reply, 'And you think that souls, like herrings, cannot be cured without smoke.'

It is the great expansion into the slums of our cities that I want to try to derive a few lessons from, but let us first think about the extent of that extraordinary surge of heroism and look at one or two of its greatest figures. If the archetypical Anglo-Catholic parish was St Alban's, Holborn in London, the archetypical address is surely found in St John, New Brunswick. When the Anglo-Catholic Movement set up shop there it hung its biretta, characteristically, on Paradise Row, an unpaved alley near the docks. The Mission Church, as it came to be called, was built at the tram terminus, so that the locals called it the last stop before Rome. I've seen the old pictures of those early days and they evoke visions of other congregations in many another Paradise Row. Whether it is Old St Paul's in Edinburgh, St James in Vancouver, St Alban's Holborn or St Peter's London Docks, the place and spirit were the same: a joyous martyrdom of self in the service of the poor to the glory of God. They would go into the back streets and the thieves' kitchens and the red-light districts and build churches of great beauty and numinous power, and they would gather round them the poor and teach them to love the Blessed Sacrament and show them how to swing a thurible. They would set up dispensaries for the sick and co-operatives and guilds, dozens of guilds. There would be fresh air camps in the country at the homes of bemused relatives for their beloved scamps from the city. There would be battles with politicians and brewers and land-lords. There would be the constant celebration of a defiantly incarnational religion. But the power and the glory of the whole movement did not lie in its often uproarious ceremonial excesses, amusingly and usually erroneously reported in the press. (You know the sort of thing from the local newspaper: 'At solemn vespers of the blessed sacrament at St Agnes by the Gasworks Anglican Church, the Holy Communion was carried in a golden

137

monster, while six thurifers, emitting thick clouds of incest, were swung round the outside of the Church. An outraged passerby said that they should not be allowed to commit celibacy in public because it scared the horses'.) No, the glory and the power of the movement lay in the quality of the priests who gave themselves to it. Cardinal Newman used to say that in missionary and evangelistic work in parish churches the clever priest got the best results in the short run, but it was the holy priest who got the best results in the long run. Let me celebrate two of the great slum priests of the Catholic Revival in a few remarks and then try to draw some lessons for today.

First, let me say something about Canon Laurie of Old St Paul's in Edinburgh. He died in 1937 after fifty years in Old St Paul's, forty of them as Rector. He'd never worked anywhere else, apart from a spell as a chaplain to the British Army during World War 1. Old St Paul's was set in the midst of the densest, if most picturesque slum in Europe, in Edinburgh's Royal Mile. By a combination of supernatural piety and straightforward social work, Laurie wrapped the poor of the city of Edinburgh round his heart. When he died, the city fathers had to stop the traffic in all the streets round the church, so dense was the crowd of mourners. He's still remembered vividly, and when I became Rector of Old St Paul's in 1968 I could sense his presence round the place, and I longed to spend a day with him back in his own time, to see him on his knees in the dark church late at night and early in the morning; to follow him up the stairs of a close in the Canongate at five in the morning to light an old lady's coal fire, because she was sick in bed; to see him at the altar, quiet and humble before his Lord in the Blessed Sacrament; to see him going his rounds in the Royal Mile, surrounded by children, for whom he kept handfuls of sweets in his trouser pockets. Above all, I wanted to see his love for his people, which was still an almost tangible thing when I was there. He lost a lot of his boys in World War 1, and he came back from the front, himself a hero, having spent most of his time crawling around in no-man's land between the trenches, comforting and praying with the dying. He built a chapel at Old St Paul's in their memory and called it the Warriors' Chapel, and he put the names of all his boys on the wall — about 170 of them. And he was often discovered late at night in the dark chapel, swinging a small censer before those columns of names, telling them over, remembering them, bearing them in his heart before God, like Moses.

Then there was Arthur Stanton, for fifty years assistant curate at St Alban's Holborn, yet at his end one of the most famous men of his generation. No intellectual, but a great preacher, an Anglo-Catholic who took Spurgeon as his homiletical model. And how he was loved, especially by the poor and more especially by the undeserving poor. What was said of St Frances de Sales — if you wished to secure his friendship, you had only to do him an injury — could be said of Arthur Stanton. He was called Dad by his parishioners. When one of them begged a shilling and Dad refused it, he clinched his argument with the reason, 'It was I, Dad, who sneaked your watch'. Fr Stanton looked at him silently for a minute and then said, 'Well, I think that does deserve a bob', and gave it to him. Here are a few more Stanton stories. Amongst many more or less distinguished persons who came to his room to visit him, came one day Mr Kensit the elder. He, like the rest, had felt the charm of the Father's preaching. He came, on this occasion, to try to snatch him from the burning, to detach him from the cause which he himself so deeply hated and so completely misunderstood. He had brought with him a roll containing drawings of various instruments of penance — 'disciplines,' chains, hair-shirts, and the like. 'These,' he said, 'are the devices by which the miserable priests seek to enslave silly women.' Father Stanton examined the roll for a minute or two; then looking up at Mr Kensit asked, with much earnestness, 'Where can I buy them? They are the very things for our ladies. Would do them a world of good.'

Even Mr Kensit must have been betrayed into the flicker of a smile. On another day, one of his old lads who had moved to the south of the Thames came to see him. He told Dad that he now thought St Alban's was quite Protestant. 'You should see what we do over at --- . Why, last Sunday evening we had sixty candles on the Altar!' 'Oh!' said Father Stanton, 'that is nothing to us!' 'Well Dad, and what do you do?' 'We, we have a clergyman that takes snuff.'

After a lifetime spent in the slums of Holborn he died in 1913. In his biography you can see photographs of the thousands who accompanied his funeral procession through the streets of London, especially the poor postal workers, to whom he had a special ministry.

These men were known in their generation, but there were countless others who were not, yet who laboured just as well, just as heroically, so that, in Scott Holland's words, 'The Old Leaders still left, Pusey and Keble, found themselves justified, more than they had ever dreamed possible, in their gallant belief that the Church was alive, and was spiritual, and could become, indeed, the Mother of the broken and poor. It was a magnificent rally of a Cause, expelled from its own native home only to win a larger victory elsewhere'. And what can we learn from all this? Well, I speak mainly for myself in what I want to say in conclusion. I am more and more troubled by the gap between our Christian profession of belief and the actual reality of our lives. The Christian faith is about sacrifice and loss and heroism. It is about a God who loved the world so much that he gave his only begotten Son, and that fact of self-emptying has always been the hallmark of authentic Christianity. We see it especially in the great call to the monastic life, with its counsels of poverty, celibacy and obedience. We see it when men and women are led to offer themselves in service to the poor of the world. And we see it in the quieter heroism that characterizes the ordinary life lived for God. I may be wrong, but I do not see much of that heroism or self-abandonment in today's Church. This is called 'the Me Generation' in America. People are, as they say, 'into' themselves. There is a great lust for self-discovery and self-pleasing, and self-gratification, and a tragic forgetting of the wisdom of Christ that says that only in losing ourselves, giving ourselves away, do we find ourselves. I fear that we are all part of the Me Generation. We don't really follow Christ. Christ is a lion who ought to thrill and terrify us. Instead, we have domesticated him and brought him into our cosy church parlours like a nice, affectionate pussy cat. It is a truly horrifying thing we have done. We have taken the vast and wintry summons of God, the great organ note of self-abandonment that sounds through the Bible, and we have put it on tape, and we let it play through our stereo system while we get on with our own little tasks about the house. The Lord has roared from Zion, and we are content because we got it on cassette.

Am I wrong? Are we not a cosy Church today? A Church without heroes. A Church with the dangerous element removed: decaffeinated Christianity. The Me Church.

There is only one hope for us in our corruption. I take enormous comfort from the fact that the apostles too were slow and unimaginative men who took a long time before they understood; and after they understood took a long time to find the courage to go the way Christ wanted to lead them. That must be our way. Not for us the way of magnificent sacrifice; but there is still left the way of small sacrifices. Giving our life to him bit by tiny bit. A bit more of our money. A bit more of our time in costly prayer. A bit more of our heart as we find small ways of loving him in others. And slowly we'll learn to give ourselves away. And maybe one day, when we are old, we'll discover that we have, after all, given all our riches away and with relief we'll run at last into the Kingdom of Heaven.

Notes

INTRODUCTION: The Rock and the River

1. G.G. Coulton, *Medieval Panorama*, Cambridge University Press, 1949, p. 349.
2. Thomas Babington Macaulay, *Critical and Historical Essays*, vol. 2, J.M. Dent, London, 1910, p. 18.
3. T.S. Eliot, *Little Gidding* in *The Complete Poems and Plays*, Harcourt, Brace and Company, New York, 1952, p. 145.

PART ONE   Suffering: An Exploration

1. The Land of Lost Content
1. A.E. Housman, *Poetry and Prose: A Selection*, Hutchinson, London, 1972, p. 86.
2. William Shakespeare, Sonnet 30.
3. Dylan Thomas, *The Poems*, J.M. Dent and Sons, London, p. 208.
4. Jean-Paul Sartre.

2. The Valley of Decision
1. Horace, *Odes*, XIV.1, translation by Richard Harris Barham.
2. William Blake, *Auguries of Innocence*.
3. Robert Browning, *Faith and Unfaith*.
4. W.B. Yeats, *The Second Coming*.
5. John Hick, *Evil and the God of Love*, Harper and Row, New York, 1966, p. 319.
6. John Milton, *Paradise Lost*, bk. XII, 1:641.

3. **A Death in Jerusalem**
   1. Charles Williams, *Descent into Hell*, Faber & Faber, London, 1949, p. 189.
   2. W.H. Vanstone, *The Stature of Waiting*, Darton Longman and Todd, London, 1982.
   3. Robert Hugh Benson, *Initiation (1914)*, p. 61, cited by Glen Cavaliero in *Charles Williams: Poet of Theology*, Macmillan Press, London, 1983, p. 82.

PART TWO   The Christian and the Sexual Revolution

4. **What Is Sex For?**
   1. Robinson Jeffers, 'The Excesses of God,' in *Be Angry at the Sun*, Random House, New York, 1941, p. 104.

5. **The Christian Answer**
   1. Rose Macaulay, *The Towers of Trebizond*, A.D. Peters and Co., London.

6. **Putting Asunder**
   1. Jonathan Gathorne-Hardy, *Marriage, Love, Sex and Divorce*, Summit Books, New York, 1981.

PART THREE   Priest to the World

7. **Looking Towards Jesus**
   1. George Tyrrell, *Christianity at the Crossroads*, George Allen and Unwin, London, 1963, p. 49.

8. **The Perfect Priest**
   1. Geoffrey Faber, *Jowett*, Harvard University Press, 1957, p. 122.

9. **The Folly of Preaching**
   1. Reinhold Niebuhr, *Leaves from the Notebook of a Tamed Cynic*, Living Age Books, New York, 1960, p. 112.

EPILOGUE: Paradise Row

1. Henry Scott Holland, *A Bundle of Memories*, Wells Gardner, Darton & Co. Ltd., London, 1915, p. 95.